Theology
as a
way of
Thinking

A *Joint Publication of*
The American Academy of Religion
and Society of Biblical Literature

Volume I
Theology as a way of Thinking
by
Richard Grigg

—

Theology as a way of Thinking

RICHARD GRIGG

Scholars Press
Atlanta, Georgia

Theology as a way of Thinking

by
Richard Grigg

Library of Congress Cataloging in Publication Data

Grigg, Richard, 1955-
    Theology as a way of thinking / by Richard Grigg.
        p.   cm. -- (Ventures in religion ; no. 01)
    Includes bibliographical references.
    ISBN 1-55540-275-5 (alk. paper). -- ISBN 1-55540-535-5 (pbk. :
alk. paper)
    1. Theology--Methodology. 2. Theology--20th century. I. Title.
II. Series.
BR118.G67   1990
230'.01--dc20   90-44089
                                                       CIP

Printed in the United States of America
on acid-free paper

To
Orval Bohner
and
Andrew Grigg

"Man thinks, God laughs."
　　　—Jewish proverb

Contents

Series
Foreword

American culture broadly assumes that the term religion properly refers to a distinct domain of human behavior, thought, and experience. The American Constitution—which guarantees freedom of and from religion as a fundamental right—assumes religion as a given. Americans generally accept the idea that it is natural for people to have a religion and that being religious is a legitimate way to live.

Another way of putting this is to say that in American life religion is a native category. It is a basic classification that our culture routinely uses to sort out and organize the complexity of human existence. We conceive religion as an unquestioned aspect of human experience. It is an ordinary component of the way Western, and especially American, culture understands the world.

Because religion is a native category, we use it both abstractly and concretely. As an abstraction—much like the categories of "language" or "culture"—religion is a concept, a theoretical entity, that helps us to identify, label, and make sense of the discrete particulars of our own or other cultures. But, like all native categories, religion also claims to be concrete, self-evident, and inherently significant. Consequently, it is evocative but inarticulate. Our culture takes religion for granted as a meaningful and conventional trait of human being, but we grasp and employ religion intuitively more than we discern and deploy it discursively. We apprehend religion better than we comprehend it. As a culture, Americans seem to know that religion is important even when we cannot explain why. We think better *with* religion than we do *about* it.

The givenness of religion in American culture explains why it is important for Americans to study religion at some point in their education. To be sure, studying religion provides an interesting entry into the lives and cultures of other people. But, equally important, the study of religion gives us some needed perspective on ourselves by helping us question what is most familiar to us—our own native categories, the cultural lenses through which we see the world.

Ventures in Religion was created with just these issues in mind. It is a series of teaching books designed to spell out, for students across a wide institutional and educational spectrum, the issues of description, analysis, and interpretation that predominate in the study of religion. The series does not provide general introductions to discrete religions or to particular religious texts or artifacts. Rather, its volumes examine persisting questions, problems, concepts, and categories that have preoccupied the study of religion and helped to constitute it as a separate field of inquiry.

The series aims to show how the study of religion formulates and solves problems, how it shapes and directs intellectual curiosity. Thus, each volume focuses on what students of religion ask and how we ask it, on what we think and why we think it, and on why our questions and answers matter. The series attempts to address both the "What?" and the "So What?" of the study of religion.

Although volumes in the series supply basic information students need, they are neither conventional textbooks nor extended encyclopedia articles. Rather, each is written as an argumentative essay—a sustained statement of reasoned opinion and judgment—that encourages readers to think critically and to take a position. Books in this series are meant to be argued with and argued about. To that end, they are books readers should feel free to write in, with space on each page to do just that.

Because the volumes of *Ventures in Religion* are problem-centered or topic-centered, they can be used, singly or together, to complement the standard textbooks in religion, which often focus on specific traditions or texts. The editors hope that the series as a whole will be sufficiently flexible to respond to the varied interests and emphases of a wide range of instructional and institutional contexts.

Ventures in Religion is the first series jointly sponsored by the *American Academy of Religion* and the *Society of Biblical Literature* designed specifically for classroom use. As such, it signals a recognition by both learned societies of the importance of teaching in the intellectual life of the field. Indeed, the series may be understood as an acknowledgment that the future of the study of religion depends on the mutual stimulation and reinforcement of good scholarship and good teaching.

William Scott Green
University of Rochester

Preface

What does one learn when one studies "theology"? That is the question which this book explores and seeks to answer. The route of our exploration will require that we steer a course between two familiar landmarks in the literature about theology: we shall undertake neither a survey of theology, on the one hand, nor what theologians like to call a "prolegomenon" to theology, on the other. Surveys introduce students to a wide range of thinkers, but they seldom point to any fundamental methodological principles to which all of the thinkers adhere. Prolegomena tend to be idiosyncratic proposals about some method theology allegedly should employ but presently does not; they reveal little about the actual practice of theological thinking. By contrast, our approach will be to describe a number of broad methodological principles and then to investigate how various theologians actually employ them. The theologians we shall consider represent a diversity of perspectives, and the sort of theology we shall explore is not tied to any one religious tradition.

It seems to me that the particular methodological principles that will be discussed in this book are necessary, and perhaps sufficient, to guarantee theology a place among the contemporary academic disciplines. This is an important issue, and the book will attempt to present theology in nonconfessional, academic terms. But these crucial methodological principles will be derived not from pronouncements by persons who seek to guard the boundaries of the academic world, but from the internal demands of theology itself and from the demands of the larger culture in which we live.

The demands internal to theological thinking will be discussed in Chapter One, the demands of modern and postmodern culture in Chapter Two. It is in Chapter Three that we shall investigate how specific instances of theological thinking exemplify the principles derived from such demands. We shall discover that, despite their common adherence to certain fundamental methodological rules, the various theologies under investigation issue in significantly different perspectives upon the divine. Chapter Four will describe some of the possible responses to this theological pluralism. Finally, in Chapter Five we shall briefly consider the question,

"Why does theology matter? Why should we engage in theological thinking?"

When writing a teaching book such as this one it is important to have access to the insights of others who teach about theology and related disciplines, and I am grateful to those colleagues who took the time to read an earlier version of the book and to comment upon it: Dennis Bielfeldt, Walter Brooks, Barbara Fischer, Steve Gowler, Joseph Grau, Edward Papa, Michael Raposa, Robert Scharlemann, and James Wieland. My conversations with these persons were a source not only of insight but also of genuine pleasure.

Chapter 1

What Is Theology?

The word "theology" derives from the Greek *theos*, which means god, and *logos*, which means word or reason. If it is broadly construed as any kind of talk or reasoning about the divine, then theology must be deemed a familiar and probably inevitable product of the human spirit. Human beings are prone to ask themselves whether they exist within some larger framework of meaning, and reflection about a god or gods is directed precisely to that question. Only the most unimaginative among us go through life without ever engaging in theological reflection of this sort.

The goal of our investigation, however, is to understand a different species of theology, namely, theology as a disciplined way of thinking that merits a place in the contemporary college and university. It will soon become apparent that this is no easy task. Is there a kind of theology that deserves a place among the contemporary academic disciplines? If so, how are we to recognize it? How can it be distinguished from the myriad other forms of talk and reflection about the divine?

If we are to satisfactorily answer these questions, we must define the terms we shall be using and spell out the criteria we shall be employing. Thus, our investigation begins with an analysis of the *theos* and *logos* of the special sort of theology we seek. What is to be understood, first of all, by the word *theos* or "god"? While the individual theologian may be free to conceive of *theos* in very specific or even idiosyncratic terms, we are looking for a broad definition that will mark out the boundaries of theology as a discipline. The challenge here is to find a definition that is neither so general as to be vacuous nor so narrow as to exclude notions that ought not to be excluded from the arena of theological inquiry.

The principle we shall attempt to follow is this: *theos* ought to be defined as precisely as possible given the proviso that the resultant notion of *theos* must be consistent with the diverse notions of ultimate reality found in the various world religions. Thus, the meaning of "god" or *theos* cannot be specified so precisely that it is at odds with the Jewish or Christian God, the Muslim Allah, the Buddhist Nirvana, the Taoist Tao, or the Hindu Brahman. To look to the world religions for our criterion of breadth is to recognize that it is the world's religious traditions, as distinguished from other cultural phenomena, that have provided humankind with the most sustained reflection on the divine.

The proviso that many, if not all, of the world religions be embraced assures the inclusiveness of our definition of *theos*. But doesn't it make precision impossible? In other words, are not the notions of ultimacy found in the various world religions sufficiently different from one another that for *theos* to cover all of them it can have no real meaning at all? Not necessarily, for the following definition of *theos* seems consistent with a good many of the world religions and yet has a definite and significant content: *theos* is that infinite dimension of reality that can deliver human beings from certain fundamental threats that result from the fact that human being is finite being. The most basic kind of infinity attributed to *theos* is the infinity it possesses just insofar as it has the power to overcome dilemmas associated with human finitude.

This definition distinguishes the particular infinity of *theos* from infinity in general. Note, for example, that the set of real numbers is infinite, but that its infinity cannot be the infinity that our definition specifies, for the infinity of the set of real numbers has no power to deliver human beings from the dilemmas associated with their finitude. Our definition specifies not some kind of infinite substance or limitless thing, but a power that must be deemed infinite because its effect upon human beings is to counter threats built into the very nature of finite existence.

Furthermore, we can add specificity to our proposed notion of *theos* by indicating precisely which sorts of threats are involved in human finitude. Paul Tillich provides a useful analysis of these threats in his book, *The Courage to Be*.[1] Tillich echoes other thinkers in his claim that the fundamental threats we encounter because of our finitude are presented to human consciousness as anxiety. Anxiety is a state of mind that is to be distinguished from fear. Fear always has a definite object: I am afraid of some particular danger, such as a vicious dog, an icy road, or the possibility of financial ruin. By contrast, anxiety has no definite object, yet it makes us conscious of a real threat. Or, to put it another way, anxiety does have an object, but that object is nothingness. Anxiety is a mood that makes us aware of a threat to our very essence as human beings; it alerts us to the threat of nonbeing, the threat that our being may be undermined or eroded.

There are, says Tillich, three major types of anxiety: ontic anxiety, moral anxiety, and spiritual anxiety. While each anxiety has both a relative and an absolute form, the absolute form determines each anxiety, for the relative form always points to the absolute form. The absolute form is always present in the background. The relative form of ontic anxiety is the anxiety of fate, the anxiety about my being thrown into existence and buffeted about by forces which I can neither predict nor comprehend and over which I have no control. The absolute form of ontic anxiety is the anxiety of death (the adjective "ontic" is derived from the Greek *on*, which means being, and is appropriate to designate an anxiety that communicates a threat to my very existence). Moral anxiety focuses on the sense that I am not the person that I ought to be, that my actual way of existing falls short of my real essence. It is subdivided into the anxiety of guilt and the anxiety of condemnation. Spiritual anxiety is subdivided into the anxiety of emptiness and the anxiety of meaninglessness. In its absolute form, spiritual anxiety has to do with the absence of a core meaning around which my life can be organized, the lack of any ultimate concern.

The three forms of anxiety often interpenetrate. For instance, the awareness that life inevitably ends in death leads some persons to conclude that life is meaningless, that it is absurd. This suggests that ontic anxiety can lead to spiritual anxiety. In a parallel fashion, moral anxiety may engender spiritual anxiety: if I feel that I have destroyed the moral core of my being by engaging in some terrible act of evil, I may decide that I have forfeited the possibility of finding any meaning in life.

Tillich asserts that all persons and all societies must deal with each of the three forms of anxiety, but he points out that one of the three types of anxiety may be experienced more powerfully than the others. This is often true of a society in its later stages, where the cultural defenses against anxiety are beginning to crumble. If we were to survey Western history, for example, we would find, according to Tillich, that ontic anxiety was predominant in the latter stages of the ancient world, that moral anxiety dominated the late middle ages, and that, as it approaches its inevitable end, modern Western consciousness is most susceptible to spiritual anxiety.

Theos, then, is that infinite dimension of reality that is able to deliver human beings from ontic, moral, and spiritual anxiety and the threats to which those anxieties point. Now Paul Tillich was a Christian thinker, and it is evident that the Christian God has traditionally been conceived as a source of deliverance from precisely the kind of threats of which Tillich speaks. The Christian doctrines of divine providence and eternal life appear to be aimed at ontic anxiety, the doctrine of the Christ's atoning death on the cross at moral anxiety, and the claim that human beings are children of God at spiritual anxiety. But Tillich's analysis does not presuppose the Christian worldview. Many of the other world religions seem to be centrally concerned with at least some of these threats.

As an example, consider Buddhism, a religion that is in many respects very different from Christianity. The goal of the Buddhist quest is Nirvana, and Nirvana is a boundlessness, an infinity that one reaches through the extinction of the finite self or ego. Why should the ego be extinguished? Because the ego's desires or cravings make suffering inevitable. The Buddhist tradition explains that Siddhartha Gautama, the man who was to become the Buddha, first observed this suffering in what have come to be known as the "four passing sights." While journeying along a road, the hitherto naive young Gautama saw an old man, a sick man, a dead man, and a monk. The first three passing sights made it clear to him in just what sense life is suffering, and those three sights correspond exactly to what Tillich terms ontic anxiety. Old age and disease fall under the heading of fate, the object of the relative form of ontic anxiety, and death is the object of the absolute form of that anxiety. One might well assume that, in addition, the apparent inevitability of such suffering arouses the anxiety of emptiness and meaninglessness. Seeing the monk suggested to Gautama the possibility of withdrawing from the world as ordinarily perceived and seeking enlightenment about how to be delivered from suffering. Thus, while there can be little doubt that Buddhism and Christianity differ from one another on such central issues as the reality of the self and the nature of the infinite, their analyses of that from which the infinite must deliver us obviously overlap significantly.

The universality of the Tillichian analysis, the fact that it is not restricted to the Christian worldview, is only reenforced by comparing Christianity with a sister religion like Judaism. Here we can focus on moral anxiety. Both traditions take moral anxiety with utmost seriousness, and both agree that guilt and condemnation have to do not only with interhuman relations but especially with man and woman's relationship to God. Nonetheless, there is disagreement between these two traditions as to how moral anxiety should be addressed. The Christian analysis of the human condition suggests that sin has so impaired human nature that man and woman can only be freed from sin by an extraordinary act of divine intervention, specifically, the death of the Son of God on the cross. Judaism disagrees, holding that human beings are always free to turn back to God of their own accord; the Christian view of human nature is overly pessimistic. Yet God is an essential element in the Jewish view, for the way back to God, the way to live one's life in harmony with God, is spelled out in the Torah, the teaching that God has revealed. Thus, despite their differing positions, both traditions recognize moral anxiety as pointing to a fundamental threat to human being, and both assume that the infinite is an essential ingredient in defining what moral failure is and in overcoming it.

It should be added that the deliverance that the world religions seek via *theos* is not simply a matter of escape but also a matter of fulfillment. To be delivered from ontic, moral, and spiritual anxiety and the threats to which they point means to experience life instead of death, forgiveness or moral purity instead of condemnation, purposefulness or bliss instead of meaninglessness. This positive side of the religious quest, and hence of the function of the infinite or *theos,* is expressed clearly by Leo Baeck in his assertion that "religion is the realization of life. In religion life finds its natural growth from the soil in which it was created and toward the end for which it was formed. In religion man attains his true self. . . ."[2]

We are using the word *theos* or "god" to mean an infinite dimension of reality that can deliver us from the fundamental threats that result from our human finitude, threats clearly articulated by Paul Tillich in his description of ontic, moral, and spiritual anxiety. What about *logos*? If the word *logos* means reason or word, then its being attached to *theos* suggests that theology involves thinking about and speaking about the infinite. Indeed, the particular species of theology we are seeking to define is theology as a disciplined way of thinking that merits a place among the contemporary academic disciplines.

Theology as such a way of thinking can be defined by a tripartite formula: the theologian (1) must provide a clear account (2) of precisely what he or she knows about the infinite (3) and of just how he or she knows it. We shall consider each part of the formula in turn.

What is meant, first of all, by providing a clear account? Most obviously, this means that it is incumbent upon the theologian to explain his or her position. The notion of explanation always implies someone to whom the explanation is offered. In certain circumstances, one might regard thinking as involving explaining something to oneself, but the kind of account intended by our formula requires that the explanation be to someone else. Giving an *account* means *being accountable* to other persons. It means giving one's thinking over to others for their scrutiny. The theologian must employ a frame of reference that is not his or hers alone, but one that is available to other people as well, so that others are able to comprehend and also to evaluate the position. In fact, we must go so far as to say that giving an account and being accountable mean employing a frame of reference that is not limited even to a particular group of people, but employing one that is, at least in principle, available to all intelligent persons.

There are both external and internal reasons for demanding this universal accountability. One of the external demands derives from the college and university. We are looking for a brand of theology that can be considered a legitimate academic endeavor, and academe requires, or at least claims to require, this kind of universal accountablity. We shall explore another external demand, one rooted in the development of modern industrial society, in the next chapter.

But perhaps the internal demand is more important, just insofar as it is internal. Theology claims to speak about that infinite dimension of reality that can deliver the kind of being we know as human being from fundamental threats associated with its finitude. Thus, theology has to do not with something peculiar to the experience of a particular individual or a particular group, but with human being as such, with what we might call "human nature." And it has to do with an infinity which, to the extent that it is genuinely infinite and transcends the finitude of human being, cannot possibly be the possession of particular individuals, but must be conceived as an essential component of reality as a whole.

In defining *theos*, we looked to the world religions, for we noted that they have provided the context for the most sustained reflection on the divine. What happens when we attempt to apply the demand for universal accountability to the various religious traditions? Here we encounter a tension. On the one hand, all of the world religions would seem to be bearers of the internal demand for universal accountability, for they speak about the human condition as such and point to the infinite that transcends human finitude. But, on the other hand, religious traditions often manifest a tendency to emphasize their own particularity. First, in order to validate their claims about the human condition and the infinite, universal themes though they be, religions often appeal to special sources of knowledge. For instance, they may say that their knowlege comes not through general reflection on the world but, rather, through a revelation contained in a sacred text. Or perhaps their alleged knowledge has been communicated to them by a particular figure whom they believe to be a manifestation of the divine. Alfred North Whitehead captures this tension when he observes, "religion claims that its concepts, though derived primarily from special experiences, are yet of universal validity, to be applied by faith to the ordering of all experience. . . . It arises from that which is special, but it extends to what is general."[3] Second, insofar as they generate all-encompassing frameworks for structuring human life, religious traditions seem to be mutually exclusive: I cannot really be a Buddhist and a Muslim at the same time, at least not as Buddhism and Islam are usually conceived. Third, to the extent that large groups of people define themselves in terms of and identify with a religion, religious traditions often become powerful social entities with political and economic significance. As such, they compete not only with one another, but also with nonreligious factions within a society. The desire to separate church and state so evident in the U.S. Constitution testifies to this third characteristic of religions.

If this tendency toward particularity on the part of religious traditions appears problematic, we must nonetheless admit that theology is intimately tied to religion. *Theos* is that infinite dimension of reality which can deliver us from fundamental threats resulting from our finitude. Religion properly can be defined as "a means toward ultimate transformation"[4], i.e., a way to transcend the threats built into human finitude. Theology attempts to gain knowledge of the infinite, while religion is the practical attempt to transcend finitude by living one's life with that same infinite in view. Thus, we can distinguish theology from religion by saying that theology is an intellectual approach to the infinite, religion an existential, personal approach. But because the infinite that theology attempts to understand is just that infinite which can aid us in dealing with fundamental practical dilemmas connected with our finitude, theological reflection tends always to point to religious practice.

What is more, it may be that the full realization of ultimate transformation, the practical appropriation of the power of the infinite, requires not just that one engage in some sort of private religious practice, but that one enter that kind of complete religious universe found only in an established religious tradition. Why? Precisely as *ultimate* transformation, the practical appropriation of the infinite involves the whole of one's experience, both the self and the world in which the self perceives itself as residing. And it may be only in the midst of a venerable religious community that one can find a symbolic and ritual apparatus that is truly complete enough to structure every moment of human life; a religious tradition provides not just tools for leading the religious life, it provides the all-encompassing environment in which that life can be lived.

What are we to make of the particularity of religions and the tie between religion and theology? The first part of the *logos* formula requires universal accountability. The theologian must make his or her case within the context of a framework of meaning and evaluation that is, in theory, accessible to all persons. The subject matter of theology must be open to all insofar as theology thinks and speaks about human nature as such and about an infinite that is an essential component of reality as a whole. But the particularity of the various religious traditions seems to resist the universalizing impetus of the *logos* formula. Perhaps each tradition should be viewed as an organic whole. Its parts will make sense in the context of that whole. Won't the parts be meaningless if removed from their organic context and evaluated according to abstract universal principles? And aren't there ways of knowing internal to such wholes, i.e., ways of knowing that are valid within a particular tradition but that will not appear valid outside it? These questions cast doubt on the validity of the principle of universal accountability.

We can defend the need for universal accountability, first, by pointing out that academic theology is not itself a religious activity. It may draw upon religious belief, or even arise as a response to religious belief, but academic theology unapologetically removes that belief from its original context and examines it from a new perspective. Thus, constraints on the drive to universality that are appropriate when one is attempting to grasp a religious tradition soely on its own terms do not apply to theology as a way of thinking.

Second, we must not overemphasize the resistance of religious traditions to the demand for universal accountability. Religions are not, in fact, totally self-contained worlds. This is especially true in modern industrial societies, where many religions exist side by side within a larger cultural whole. If religious traditions were really self-contained, then persons from two different traditions would not be able to communicate with one another at all; they would be alien species for one another. But persons from different traditions can, of course, communicate with one another, even about their different religious beliefs.

If the demand for universal accountability is valid, we must nonetheless be careful about how we conceive universality, so that we do not unnecessarily limit the scope of theological thinking. In other words, we must attempt to avoid a rigid, oppressive notion of universal principles of thinking, a notion that would claim universality for a perspective that, in reality, reflects the narrow interests of a particular group of persons. For example, some have argued that the notion of "universal reason" so dear to the advocates of the eighteenth century movement known as the Enlightenment is simply the particular kind of reason that suits the needs of white European males of the modern era. Thus, the notion of universality involved in the principle of universal accountability ought to be a flexible, expansive notion. It should allow for different kinds of "evidence" for claims about the infinite. In Chapter Three, we shall have an opportunity to explore the concrete application of the principle of universal accountability.

On the one hand, then, the sort of theology of interest to us is one that proceeds on the basis of universally available criteria of understanding and evaluation. This theology cannot be one that is valid only for those who have made a commitment to a particular religion. But, on the other hand, we have suggested that the theology we seek might well investigate the theological claims arising from a particular religious tradition. This results in the following question: can a practitioner of academic theology be, at the same time, the devotee of a particular religion? Everything depends on what is meant by "at the same time." The theologian cannot cast his or her theology in a form that can be understood and evaluated only by adherents of his or her religion. But there can be no objection to the theologian practicing a particular religion, or even to his or her theological reflection resulting from a religious commitment, as long as the theological position itself is explained and defended in the context of an intellectual framework available to those outside that religion; the theological position cannot presuppose the commitment. In fact, most of the specific theologies that we shall consider in Chapter Three arise out of a particular religious commitment, yet we shall be considering them as candidates for a genuinely academic theology.

The second part of our tripartite *logos* formula states that theologians must make clear exactly *what* they claim to know. Building on our discussion of universal accountability, we can say that the theologian's explanation of what he or she claims to know must be expressed within a conceptual framework available in principle to all intelligent persons. As for the third part of our formula, theologians must explain *how* they know what they claim to know. They must be self-conscious about how they arrive at their purported knowledge. Once again the principle of universal accountability enters in, for the *how*, i.e., the particular way of knowing the theologian claims to employ, must be a way of knowing open to all. The same distinction must be made here that was just made above. The theologian may claim knowledge via a particular text or historical event, and a particular text or historical event may not be universally familiar. But the judgment that a particular text or event provides knowledge of the infinite must be made on the basis of criteria that are universally available.

It is important to note how closely connected the second and third parts of the *logos* formula are to the first. Indeed, one might claim that the second and third flow from the first, that they are demanded by the first. To say that theologians (1) must be accountable, is to say that (2) they must be able to explain to all other intelligent persons exactly what they claim to know, and that (3) they must show how all intelligent persons could come to know this same reality. But it is also important to recognize how closely connected the second and third parts are *to one another*. The *what* and the *how* stand in a reciprocal relationship. They condition one another. For instance, suppose that one asserts, as nearly all religious thinkers would, that the infinite dimension of reality intended by the word *theos* is suprasensible, that is, that the infinite is not a material thing. This statement about the *what* of theology has an immediate bearing on the *how*, for it is obvious that if the infinite is suprasensible, we cannot come to know it simply through the five senses. The senses provide us with information about the physical world and, in and of themselves, can tell us nothing about any supraphysical reality. Given the nature of what theology claims to know, the explanation of how it knows will necessarily involve an appeal to something more than our sensory capacities.

This mutually conditioning character of the *what* and *how* of theological knowledge also means that if one were to carefully analyze how the human mind can attain genuine knowlege, one would be in a position to place certain restrictions on what theology can claim to know; how we know puts limitations on what we can know. Thus, an inventory of the human mind's capacities for knowledge would provide a kind of negative outline of the infinite about which theology can legitimately speak.

The three parts of our *logos* formula are all contained, at least in germ, in a single word that has come to play an important role in twentieth century theology. In a brilliant work that appeared posthumously in 1919, the German philosopher and religious thinker Hermann Cohen asserted that "the relation between God and man proves itself to be a *correlation*."[5] The divine can only be understood in correlation with the human. Consider how the notion of correlation squares with our tripartite formula. First, the human capacities with which the divine is to be correlated are not peculiar to members of a particular tradition but are capacities which all human beings share. This is one of the reasons that Paul Tillich, to whom we have already had reason to refer, builds his theological system around correlation: "Systematic theology uses the method of correlation. It has always done so, sometimes more, sometimes less, consciously, and must do so consciously and outspokenly, especially if the apologetic point of view is to prevail."[6] The word "apologetic" in Tillich's statement refers to the attempt to convince those who do not share one's religious convictions that those convictions are sound, that they ought to be embraced. The attempt to convince others of the truth of one's own position necessarily involves the use of a frame of reference common to oneself and the others. The method of correlation means understanding the divine in correlation with the general human condition. It is a method which includes what we have called the principle of universal accountability. In the case of Tillich's system, the general human condition is represented by the fundamental anxieties we discussed above. Thus, in his attempt to explain the Christian faith, Tillich correlates the Christian notion of God with the threat of nonbeing as communicated by ontic, moral, and spiritual anxiety: "Only those who have experienced the shock of transitoriness, the anxiety in which they are aware of their finitude, the threat of nonbeing, can understand what the notion of God means."[7] The point of course is that all human beings, given the very nature of what it means to be human, have experienced, to a greater or lesser degree, the threat of which Tillich speaks.

To correlate the divine with the human is also to clarify *what* theology claims to know. Theology attempts to grasp the infinite. But *finitum non capax infiniti*, the finite cannot grasp the infinite. Therefore, the infinite can only be understood if it is brought into some kind of relationship with our finite condition. Correlation means that the infinite is grasped via a description of how it affects human beings. We cannot know exactly what the infinite is in and of itself, but we can know what it is in its relationship to us. Thus, the great medieval theologian Moses Maimonides, who influenced Hermann Cohen's use of the method of correlation, held that the attributes of God which we can know are attributes of action, i.e., attributes that have to do with how God acts toward human beings. Some such correlative principle is implied by our definition of *theos* as the infinite dimension of reality that can deliver human beings from fundamental threats connected with their finitude.

Finally, it should be evident that to correlate the divine with the human is to explain *how* theology knows what it claims to know. We know *theos* through how it affects human being. The individual theologian will explain exactly what effects he or she believes the divine to have upon human being, and the examination of those particular effects will tell us *what* the infinite is, which means that this examination is *how* we come to know the infinite. One again we see the close connection between the *what* of theology and its *how*.

Hermann Cohen and Paul Tillich were giants of early twentieth century theology, and both spoke explicitly of correlating the divine with the human. One can find theologians writing today who also make explicit reference to the principle of correlation. For example, David Tracy, in his attempt to recommend a method for a specifically Christian theology, says that "the two principal sources for theology are Christian texts and common human experience and language." He goes on to explain that "the theological task will involve a critical correlation of the results of the investigations of the two sources of theology."[8] Similarly, another Christian theologian, Schubert Ogden, holds that "theology presupposes as a condition of its possibility the correlation of the Christian witness of faith and human existence."[9] But even if he or she does not actually use the word "correlation," any theologian who observes the meaning of the *logos* of theology as we have explained it will have to employ the principle of correlation in some fashion.[10]

We are now in a position to offer a preliminary answer to the question, "What is theology?" Theology, as *logos* about *theos*, is a disciplined way of thinking about the infinite. The infinite is the dimension of reality that can deliver human beings from certain fundamental threats connected with their finitude, threats communicated to consciousness in ontic, moral, and spiritual anxiety. To refer to theology as a disciplined way of thinking means that the theologian (1) must provide a clear account (2) of exactly what he or she knows (3) and of just how he or she knows it. This will involve correlating the infinite with the kind of being we call human being.

Our answer may, on the surface, appear to be a rather exacting blueprint for doing theology. For that reason, it is necessary to emphasize two things. First, this description of theology is anything but narrow. Recall that our definition of *theos* is meant to be consistent with diverse notions of ultimate reality. And our tripartite *logos* formula and concept of correlation put few restrictions on the sort of human capacities for knowlege that can come into play in theology. We have not demanded, for example, that theologians draw upon only those capacities recognized as legitimate in other academic disciplines. The possibility of divine revelation is not ruled out by our description of theology as a disciplined way of thinking. All that our description demands is that, however a theologian may claim to attain knowledge of the infinite, that knowlege and that way of knowing must, in principle, be open to all other intelligent persons as well, regardless of the traditions to which they do or do not belong.

Second, we must emphasize that theology as a disciplined way of thinking is not a simple and surefire method of investigation such that, if employed in mechanical fashion, it can be counted on to turn out knowledge of the divine. We have seen nothing that would indicate that knowlege of the divine is easy to come by. On the contrary, just as there are both external and internal demands for universal accountability, there are both external and internal reasons for believing that knowlege of *theos*, if it can be had at all, can only be attained with great difficulty. Some of the external reasons will be explored in the next chapter. The all-important internal reason has already been alluded to in our discussion of correlation: the object of theological investigation is the infinite, something that lies beyond not only our own finitude but the whole finite world of which we are a part. How can the finite hope to grasp the infinite? "Man thinks, God laughs." This proverb is the watchword for our investigation, and it must serve to remind us that the way of thinking that is theology can only be traversed by one who has a healthy skepticism about our ability to calculate the contours of the divine.

Thus, the phrase "theology as a way of thinking" has parallels to Martin Heidegger's notion of thinking as a way upon which one must enter if one is to understand Being.[11] Being, which Heidegger continually warns us not to confuse with beings, can never be the object of a mechanical method of investigation which seeks to cognitively manipulate reality. Indeed, the kind of thinking appropriate to Being is not a method at all, not some kind of tool at our disposal. As one Heidegger commentator puts it, drawing upon Heidegger's own vocabulary, "Thinking is not so much an act as a way of living or dwelling."[12] It is a response to Being that involves persistently asking one question after another, patiently following the many twists and turns of the pathway onto which Being has called the thinker.

One can reasonably assume, given the nature of the infinite sought by theology, that the pathway of theological thinking will have as many twists and turns as the one described by Heidegger in his quest for Being. It remains to be seen, however, whether the theological pathway will, if patiently trod, lead us to knowledge of the divine, or whether it is a dead end that will leave us stranded amidst illusion.

Modernity's Challenge to Theology

In Europe during the middle ages, Christian theology was deemed the "Queen of the Sciences."[13] All other kinds of learning paled before theology's regal splendor, for no other science aimed at such lofty topics or possessed such certainty as did the divine science. Philosophy had a status second only to that of theology; it was deemed theology's "handmaid."

The modern period seems to have turned the medieval worldview on its head: for many persons today, no kind of learning is more dubious than theology, no way of thinking more unworthy of the title "science." Consistent with this reversal, philosophy is considered a kind of ivory tower speculation that is only one rung higher on the ladder of respectability than theology. One clever critic has summed up the situation this way: What is the difference between a philosopher and a theologian? The philosopher is like a blind man who is in a totally dark room looking for a black cat that isn't there. The theologian is like a blind man who is in a totally dark room looking for a black cat that isn't there. . . and he finds it.

This description may be an exaggeration of the modern attitude, but it is no exaggeration to say that theology has witnessed a reversal of its fortunes in modernity. Theology is no longer the paradigm of secure knowledge. Instead, theology is on the defensive and must justify its claims to provide knowledge of the divine before a court of often hostile modern opinion.

In the first chapter, we discussed the internal demand for universal accountablity and the internal recognition of the difficulty of attaining knowledge of the infinite. These arose from within theology itself, given the very nature of what it purports to investigate. The present chapter is parallel to the first, in that it will focus on the external demand for accountability placed upon theology and the external skepticism about the possibility of knowing the infinite. In order to understand these external pressures, we shall have to investigate the status of religion in the modern world, for religion is the original locus of theology. Thus, we shall begin with an examination of the process of secularization. As we shall see, secularization is not simply an intellectual, philosophical phenomenon, but a process that involves nearly all dimensions of Western society. When we have completed our discussion of secularization, we can narrow our focus and investigate how modern philosophy contributes to the external demands placed upon theology.

The Secularization of the West

Secularization can be succinctly defined, in Peter Berger's words, as "the process by which sectors of society and culture are removed from the domination of religious institutions and symbols."[14] Premodern Western society was also presecular. The Christian Church and the symbols of the Christian faith dominated all sectors of society in the middle ages. Indeed, the Church, along with the political order, provided the organizing principles around which medieval society was formed.

As Robert Bellah has pointed out, premodern society in the West was organic and hierarchical.[15] That is, the different sectors of premodern society—the religious, the political, the economic, the artistic, to name but the most important—were joined together as a unified whole, just as an organism is a unified whole formed out of individual cells. And the organizing principles of the societal organism were hierarchical; there were certain overarching goals and values to which all social activities and all social sectors were subservient. It was the Christian religion, with the aid of politics, that provided the ultimate ends toward which the society was expected to strive: "the end of religion is salvation, of politics the common good."[16] Such a society can properly be termed "Christendom."

Once we grasp the Christian religion's central role in medieval society, it becomes apparent that Christian theology's status as the Queen of the Sciences was not

achieved simply on the basis of theology's own attributes. Rather, theology's status was, at least in part, a
function of the authoritative position of Christianity in
the societal organism. This does not mean, however,
that we can reduce the place of theology in medieval
society to purely extra-theological, sociological factors.
We encounter an instance of the "chicken and the egg"
dilemma at this point: does Christian theology's lofty
position result from the Christian religion's place atop
the larger societal hierarchy, or does the Christian
religion's place atop the hierarchy result from the
inherent strengths of the Christian worldview, a
worldview most clearly articulated precisely in Christian
theology? The most plausible answer is that the two
sides of the formula stand in a reciprocal relationship to
one another, i.e., that they are mutually reenforcing.
The average citizen in medieval Europe was likely to
regard the Christian worldview as convincing, if not self-
evident, given the fact that he or she existed in the midst
of a society where the organizing principles were
provided by Christianity. At the same time, the fact that
the society was so organized seemed perfectly appropriate, given the content of the Christian worldview.

All of this changes, however, with the advent of
modern industrial society, at least as early as the
seventeenth century. In modernity, the organic hierarchy of the middle ages is dissolved. Now the dominant
sector in society is the economy, not religion or the
political order. Why does this transfer of power to the
economic sector undermine the organic unity of Western
society? Because the economy does not provide the kind
of overarching social goals and values that religion and
the political order did. The goal of religion is salvation
and the goal of politics the common good, and both of
those goals can serve as ultimates that hierarchically
organize a society. By contrast, the economy generates
no goals or values that transcend itself; the goals of the
economy are purely economic and thus offer no guidance
to other sectors of society. As a result, each sector of
society tends to become autonomous from every other
sector, a law unto itself.

This process dethrones religion and theology in at
least two ways. First, it exalts a new kind of reason or
thinking. What kind of reason is required in the now
dominant economic sector? Not a reason that searches
for ultimate ends worthy of humanity, the kind of reason
employed by the theologian, but a calculative, technical
reason that aims simply to figure out the most efficient

means to an end, where the end in question is limited to economics. And as one sector of society after another follows the economy in attaining autonomy from the larger social whole, a process that is inevitable when there are no overarching principles to unify the various sectors, each sector will turn to the kind of technical, utilitarian reason exalted by the economy. Each sector will be concerned only with finding the most efficient means for accomplishing ends immanent to that particular sector.

The exaltation of this technical reason helps to explain not only why theology has been removed from its throne in modernity but also why natural science has taken theology's place as the paradigm of genuine knowledge. Natural science is technical reason par excellence. It is perceived as a wholly autonomous realm where no extrinsic principles are allowed to intrude. Thus, we are often told that the natural sciences are "value-free," meaning, on the one hand, that the scientist is expected to practice total objectivity, bracketing any personal, subjective commitments that he or she may have, and, on the other hand, that the natural sciences themselves are concerned only with the pursuit of knowledge for knowlege's sake and therefore have no value implications. The natural sciences provide, as Berger would have it, "an autonomous, thoroughly secular perspective on the world."[17]

Of course, here too we must speak of a reciprocal relationship. The prestigious place of natural science in the modern world is due in large part to the dynamics of secularization going on in the larger society. But science, in turn, surely has an influence on the larger society and the dynamics of secularization. The spectacular and undeniable successes of science in its attempt to understand the world around us reenforce the plausibility of the kind of autonomous, technical reason associated with modern secular society.

If there is a conflict between theology and the natural sciences in modernity, it has to do principally with the dispute about what kind of thinking produces knowledge. Natural science is now the paradigm of valid knowledge, and it rests on principles such as the appeal to empirically available data (i.e., data that is, at least indirectly, observable to the senses) and the ability to conclusively verify or falsify hypotheses in the laboratory. To the degree that theology cannot employ these principles, its claim to knowledge is often regarded as problematic or even as totally bogus. In other words, the most serious disagreement between theology and natural science has to do not with differences of opinion on particular matters of fact —one thinks of the dispute between conservative Christianity and Darwin's theory of the evolution of the species, a dispute symbolized by the Scopes "Monkey Trial"—but on the formal, methodological issue of how one attains valid knowlege.

Insofar as modern society opts for technical, utilitarian reason as the proper avenue to knowledge, with natural science representing the purest form of such reason, modernity is suspicious of theology's claim to provide knowledge of an infinite dimension of reality. Here is one important source of what we have called the external skepticism about the possibility of coming to know the infinite. As we have seen, there is also an internal skepticism about such knowlege, a skepticism which arises from within theology itself. But the external recognition of the difficulty of coming to knowlege of the divine will prove much more problematic for theology than the internal, as we shall see below when we turn from our sociological analysis to a consideration of modern philosophy.

Secularization dethrones religion and theology first of all by exalting a new kind of reason. A second important way in which the processes at work in modernity have undermined the role of theology is by "privatizing" religion. We have seen that religion was a unifying force in medieval society. It was deemed to have relevance to all other sectors of society. But what happens to religion when the modern industrial world places the economy in the center of things and the social organism breaks apart into autonomous units? Religion no longer has an all-encompassing relevance, an authority that is exercised over the entire society. Instead, because each sector of society is now autonomous and hence insulated against religious interference, religion itself becomes a matter of purely private concern. Its influence is restricted to the private dimensions of one's being. Berger puts it this way: "a businessman or politician may faithfully adhere to the religiously legitimated norms of family life, while at the same time conducting his activities in the public sphere without any reference to religious values of any kind. It is not difficult to see that such segregation of religion within the private sphere is quite 'functional' for the maintenance of the highly rationalized order of modern economic and political institutions."[18] Modern institutions are "rationalized" just to the degree that they employ an autonomous, utilitarian form of reasoning.

An important correlate of the privatization of religion is the phenomenon called "pluralism." Modern society is pluralistic in that a plurality of religions can exist side by side, no one of them being regarded as mandatory or authoritative for society as a whole. Religion is a purely private affair. Thus, it is left up to each individual which religion, if any, he or she should choose to adopt. There is no longer one "official" religion sanctioned by the society; Christendom is a thing of the past. It follows that each religion must compete with all other religions for adherents in what amounts to a free market. Religions must sell themselves in the same way that a business must sell its products.[19] And here we see one source of the external demand for universal accountability that modern society imposes upon theology. Religious beliefs and, by extension, theological positions are no longer mandatory. If theologians wish to have others accept their theological positions, they must market those positions. Theology must appeal to its potential consumers, and this entails adopting a framework for understanding and evaluation that is available, in principle, to all of those potential consumers and not just to the particular group or tradition from out of which the theological position in question originally grew.

While we have been analyzing secularization in terms of the demise of Christendom, secularization obviously has important implications for non-Christian religions and theologies as well. Since the other tradition most important for our purposes is Judaism, we must consider the effects of secularization on Judaism. Here we encounter a paradox: while Judaism occupied a position in medieval Europe that was in many ways exactly opposite the one enjoyed by Christianity, the theological results were similar. Because Christianity was the officially sanctioned religion of medieval society and the unifying focus of the social organism, Jews found themselves in the position of a persecuted minority. Jews were excluded from the mainstream of society, and they were often huddled together in ghettos: "from about the year 1500, the Jewish residential quarter of a city was walled in and its gates were locked from sundown to sunrise."[20] But this isolation of the Jewish community from the rest of society made the Jewish worldview the only real option for the inhabitants of the ghetto. In other words, except for periodic attempts on the part of Christians to convert Jews, the Jewish worldview found itself in a position vis-a-vis the inhabitants of the Jewish ghetto not entirely unlike the position of the Christian worldview vis-a-vis the larger Christian society. Both were protected, to a large extent, from competition and hence from the need to vigorously defend themselves intellectually, though Jews of course had to defend themselves in every other way, including physically, from the hostile Christian majority.

Modernity brought Christendom to an end. Religious allegiance became a matter of purely private concern. As a result, Jews experienced what has come to be called the "Emancipation": Jews were admitted, at least to some extent, into the societal mainstream. One advocate of this Emancipation in France, Clermont Tonnere, clearly expressed its rationale by declaring, "To the Jews as a nation we must deny everything. To the Jews as individuals we must grant everything."[21] In other words, the Emancipation is not a matter of giving some kind of official recognition to Judaism or to the Jewish people as a group. Rather, it is a result of the dismantling of Christendom and the privatization of religion.

From the point of view of advocates of the Jewish worldview, the Emancipation must be considered a mixed blessing. For now that worldview must enter into direct competition with other religious and theological positions, not to mention secular forms of reason such as the natural sciences. The secularization of Western culture means that Jews must live amidst the same pluralism as Christians have to contend with. The Jewish worldview, like the Christian, has to be marketed, and it is now quite possible for someone born into the Jewish community to opt for some other religion or for no religion at all. Jewish thought too has to contend with the external demand for universal accountability and the external skepticism about the possibility of attaining knowledge of the infinite.

Philosophy's Challenge to Theology

Our investigation of secularization has shown how the external demand for universal accountability and the external skepticism about the possibility of grasping the infinite arise out of the general societal dynamics of the modern period. We can now turn our attention to theology's perennial dialogue-partner, philosophy, and explore how modern philosophy reenforces and adds specificity to these external challenges.

What is the relationship between modern philosophy and the dynamics of the larger society in which it is situated? It is possible to read the development of modern philosophy as a purely intraphilosophical affair. Thus, problems inherent in the "rationalism" of philosophers such as Descartes, Leibniz, and Spinoza result in the countervailing "empiricism" of thinkers like Locke and Hume. The clash between the rationalist and empiricist schools leads, in turn, to the thought of the greatest of all modern philosophers, Immanuel Kant.

But it is also possible to see developments in modern philosophy as, in part, a response to the larger social environment of modernity. As we noted in the opening paragraphs of this chapter, many moderns believe that philosophy is only a bit less problematic than theology. Philosophy too has had to adapt itself to a world in which the paradigm of secure knowledge is provided by the natural sciences, rather than by the kind of speculation with which philosophy is often associated. And while there is nothing to be gained by interpreting modern philosophy as simply a product of its social environment, it is instructive to observe that the most important philosopher of the modern period did regard the natural science of his day, along with mathematics, as the model of valid knowledge. It is his thought which we must now investigate.

Immanuel Kant's most influential work, the *Critique of Pure Reason*, appeared in 1781. Its subject matter is epistemology, the study of how we attain knowledge. Kant engages in a "transcendental" analysis: he seeks to uncover *the conditions of the possibility* of genuine knowlege. Kant assumes that in order to understand how we know things, we must uncover the presuppositions or preconditions of the knowing process. This transcendental analysis of the *how* of human knowing has direct implications for the *what* of our knowing as well. In fact, Kant's work is a "critique" precisely insofar as, via an analysis of how we know, it sets definite limits to what we can know; it critiques the pretensions of human reason.

We cannot very well uncover the conditions that make valid knowledge possible unless we already have some sense of what valid knowledge is. What does Kant choose as an ideal example of genuine knowlege? The physics of Isaac Newton represents, for Kant, the epitome of the human mind's attempt to know the world. If we can uncover the conditions that make possible the judgments of Newtonian physics, we shall be in a position to determine just how the human mind can attain knowledge.

One of the central components of Newton's physics is the principle of causality: every change or event has a cause. A familiar example of causality is provided by the motion of billiard balls. Suppose that billiard ball "a" rolls toward a stationary ball, "b." The instant after ball "a" hits ball "b," ball "b" begins to move. All of us would be inclined to say that the collision of "a" with "b" *caused* billiard ball "b" to move. But, following in the footsteps of the Scottish philosopher David Hume, let us analyze what we actually observe when we watch the billiard balls. First, we note that there is no spatial or temporal interruption between the movement of ball "a" and the movement of ball "b;" they "touch" one another in both space and time. Second, we note that the alleged cause, the movement of ball "a," occurs prior to the alleged effect, the movement of ball "b." Third, no matter how many times we see ball "a" hit ball "b," we note that in every case ball "b" then begins to move; there is a constant conjunction between the collision of the balls and the movement of ball "b."

Does our observing these three phenomena constitute an observation of causality? No, says Hume, for there is one thing missing, necessary connection. Even if we have repeated the experiment a thousand times, all we can claim is that, on the particular occasions when we performed the experiment, when ball "a" hit ball "b," ball "b" began to move. How do we know that this is anything more than coincidence? How do we know that the movement of the one ball and the movement of the other are necessarilly connected? We cannot actually observe necessary connection: we do not see anything that means the movement of the two balls *must* be connected, that it would be impossible for them not to be connected. Yet unless there is such a necessary connection, it seems we cannot speak of a causal relationship, we cannot say that the collision of ball "a" with ball "b" *caused* "b" to move.

The fact remains that we do assume that events have causes. When we see billiard ball "a" collide with billiard ball "b" and ball "b" begins to move, we will assume a causal relationship, a necessary connection rather than a merely accidental juxtaposition. Why do we assume a necessaary connection if we never actually observe one? Humes's most often cited answer looks to our psychological makeup. Because in our experience the collision of the two balls is always followed by the movement of ball "b," we become conditioned to expect that to happen. We develop a habit of mentally connecting the collision of the balls with the subsequent movement of ball "b." Thus, Hume's account explains why we *assume* that there are causal relationships, but it does not allow us to grant that causal relationships actually exist.

By undermining the notion of causality, Hume's analysis challenged the status of Newtonian physics. Kant was determined to meet that challenge, and in order to do so, he had to rethink the generally accepted ideas about the relation between the human mind and the world it attempts to know. It seems quite natural to conceive of the mind as a passive instrument, like a blank tablet upon which the external world inscribes itself or a mirror which simply reflects the reality around it. But traditional, common sense ways of undertanding things sometimes need to be reversed. Kant calls to our attention the example of Copernicus: "Failing of satisfactory progress in explaining the movements of the heavenly bodies on the supposition that they all revolved round the spectator, he tried whether he might not have better success if he made the spectator to revolve and the stars to remain at rest."[22] In Kant's view, our traditional conception of the relationship between the mind and the objects it seeks to comprehend needs to undergo a kind of Copernican revolution. Instead of assuming that the mind must conform itself to the objects it wishes to know, we should entertain the hypothesis that those objects must in some sense conform themselves to the mind.

For Kant, all valid knowledge presupposes two components. First, there must be a material element, i.e., the "information" given to us by the outside world. This information comes through our senses or, in more technical language, sensible intuition. Intuition is the reception of something given to us, and Kant maintains that our knowledge requires sensible intuition, the reception of data from the outside world via the five senses.

Second—and here we get to the heart of Kant's Copernican revolution—all valid knowledge also requires a formal element, and that formal element is contributed by the mind. The data that we receive through our senses is unformed, it consists of separate bits and pieces. The mind must provide a form for the data, must organize and unify it so that it can become the object of thought. It is in this way that objects must conform to the mind. Strictly speaking, their very status as objects is a function of the mind's formal capacities.

Perhaps an analogy, even a crude one, is helpful at this point: a newspaper photograph is composed of hundreds of tiny dots. The dots themselves are analogous to the data provided by our senses. In order to constitute a picture, the dots have to be formed, they have to be organized in a particular pattern. The patterning of the dots is analogous to the imposition of form by the mind.

If the mind must always form the information given us through our senses, then we can safely say that there will be certain constant features of the world as we experience it, certain features that we know in advance will always characterize that world. They will be precisely those features that the mind contributes, the forms that the mind imposes on the data of sensible intuition. To use another, equally crude analogy: if I wear rose colored glasses, I can be certain that everything I see will be rose colored. That will be a constant of the world I experience.

This brings us to Kant's rescue of causality and, hence, of Newton's physics. According to Kant, we know that events are causally connected with one another and that they must always be so connected, for the law of cause and effect is one of the devices employed by the mind to unify the data provided by sensible intuition. Causality is not, as Hume thought, simply a matter of psychological conditioning, it is an absolutely necessary feature of the world as we experience it. Kant's Copernican revolution in philosophy amounts to showing that objects must conform to the mind, and the imposition of the law of cause and effect is one of the ways in which the mind enforces that conformity.

At first glance, Kant's critical philosophy may appear to enhance the position of the mind and thinking. After all, the mind now has the power, as it were, to demand that the world conform to our thinking. But, in reality, Kant's philosophy severely limits the powers of the mind. We have seen that our knowledge of the world always presupposes, as a condition of its possibility, two elements, the material element given to us via the senses and the formal element contributed by the mind. But this means that we can know the world only as it has been formed by the mind. We never know the world as it is in itself, but only as it appears to us after having been arranged by the mind's formal apparatus. Thus, Kant distinguishes between the "noumenal" world, which is the world as it is in itself, ever beyond our capacities to know it, and the "phenomenal" world, the world as we experience it.

Furthermore, if knowledge entails the mind arranging something given to it through the senses, we can know only those things of which we have a sensible intuition. Thinking, if done in isolation from the material provided via the senses, amounts to a mere empty play of forms. But this means that God, as an infinite reality, is something that we can never come to know, for something infinite can never be given in sensible intuition. Thus, Kant's analysis of *how* we know leads to a momentous conclusion about *what* we can know. We may be able to form an idea of God, but we can never be certain that anything in reality corresponds to that idea. The idea must always remain empty.

While Kant denies the possibility of genuine *knowledge* of God, he does allow for a subjective justification of *belief* in God. He explains that "when the holding of a thing to be true is sufficient both subjectively and objectively, it is *knowledge*." But when the holding of a thing to be true is "only subjectively sufficient, and is at the same time taken as being objectively insufficient, we have what is termed *believing*."[23] The most powerful subjective justification for affirming the existence of God is, says Kant, a moral or "practical" justification: I have to believe that God exists if I am to fulfill my moral duty, for only God can guarantee that the world in which we live is the kind of place where the moral life can succeed.

Theology as a way of thinking, however, aims at genuine knowlege of the infinite, not mere belief. And the critical philosophy of Immanuel Kant adds weight to the external skepticism about the possibility of ever coming to know the divine. One could of course choose to question Kant's starting point and to disagree with his analysis of how genuine knowlege is possible. But, for our purposes, the real significance of Kant is not contained in the specifics of his philosophy but in that philosophy's unquestionable ability to show us the crucial significance of the question about *how* we know and to uncover the interrelationship of the *how* of knowledge with the *what*. Furthermore, anyone who does decide to reject the specifics of Kant's analysis must bear the burden of providing an alternative account of how we know and what we can know. Kant's critical philosophy issues a challenge to theological thinking, and the theologian cannot simply ignore that challenge.

As Kant's philosophy illustrates, the assumption that we cannot attain genuine knowledge of God does not necessarily lead to the conclusion that there is no God. But surely it is not unreasonable for one who assumes that we cannot know anything about God to entertain the hypothesis that God does not exist. One challenge facing proponents of this hypothesis is the need to explain the origin of belief in God, to show that the belief does not possess the kind of validity that Kant's moral interpretation imparts to it.

The challenge was enthusiastically taken up in the nineteenth century by Ludwig Feuerbach. Feuerbach contended that God is an objectification of the essence of the human species. Individual men and women recognize a standard of perfection, an infinity, before which they as individuals always come up short. They mistakenly suppose that this infinite reality is a separate entity, a Supreme Being, when in fact it is nothing other than the essence of the human species, that is, the essential characteristics of the human race abstracted from their imperfect instantiation in individual human beings. Charles Hartshorne and William Reese explain Feuerbach's position this way: "If we consider, not what this or that man actually is, but all that men sometime somewhere, under some conditions or other, might be, we have (Feuerbach thinks) an unlimited scope of possible thoughts, experiences, and acts of will or of love. So, then, the omnipotence of God is really the omnipotence of man taken in this indeterminate way."[24] By believing in God, human beings are projecting outside of themselves and objectifying what is in reality their own essence. Feuerbach's philosophy paved the way for later thinkers who would work variations on his critique of theism. Karl Marx, for instance, argued that God is a projection whose origin lies in the economic substructure of society, and Sigmund Freud asserted that belief in God is the result of our desire for a cosmic protector, the human father writ large.

It will be helpful to pause at this point and take stock of what we have learned. In Chapter One, we noted how the demand for universal accountability arose from within theology, given theology's desire to speak about human being as such and about an infinite dimension of reality which transcends the whole finite world of which we are a part. This demand brought with it the need for theology to explain both the *what* and the *how* of its knowledge. The nature of theology's object also dictated a healthy skepticism about our ability to know that object. In this chapter, we have explored the origin in modern society of the external demand for universal accountability as well as the external skepticism about our ability to know the infinite. Both are rooted in the process of secularization, and both are given specificity and reenforced in the philosophy of Immanuel Kant. Kant's analysis of the *how* and the *what* of knowledge challenges theologians to supply an account of the *how* and *what* of theological knowledge and, thus, to take the demand for universal accountability seriously. The Kantian restrictions on what we can know provide a strong justification for skepticism about our possible knowledge of the divine. The external skepticism is deepened in the thought of critics of theism such as Feuerbach, Marx, and Freud.

In one sense, then, the first two chapters of our investigation of theology parallel one another. Chapter One explores the internal demand for accountability and the internal skepticism, while Chapter Two examines their external forms. But while the paths we have followed parallel one another, the destinations to which they have led us are very different, especially where the two forms of skepticism are concerned. The internal skepticism arises from a sense of the grandeur of *theos*, its distance from finite human being, while the external skepticism, at least in its sharpest form, arises from exactly the opposite sensibility, the conviction that *theos* does not exist except as a projection of human being. The internal skepticism and the external skepticism are mirror images of each other; the one completely reverses the other. The spirit of the former is expressed by the proverb "Man thinks, God laughs," the spirit of the latter by Ludwig Feuerbach's assertion that "Theology is Anthropology."[25]

From Modernity to Postmodernity

What, then, is the prognosis for theology in the

present age? Many thinkers contend that we no longer live in the modern world, but in a postmodern world. This transition from modernity to postmodernity has to do not so much with a particular point in time as with a particular intellectual perspective that crops up in various places in the nineteenth and twentieth centuries. Modernity exalted the kind of autonomous, instrumental reason associated with natural science. The confidence that modernity put in such reason is especially apparent in the seventeenth and eighteenth century intellectual movement known as the Enlightenment. Many observers, however, tend to be skeptical about this modern attitude. These postmodern thinkers suggest that moderns were deceived both about the consequences of the reason they employed and about its very nature.

It can hardly be denied that recent history has provided a powerful motive for skepticism about technical, utilitarian reason. For instance, James Cone observes that, "For black and red peoples in North America, the spirit of the Enlightenment was socially and politically demonic, becoming a pseudo-intellectual basis for their enslavement or extermination."[26] And how are we to evaluate the role of modern technical reason in Nazi Germany? There were, of course, barbarous political movements long before the advent of the modern period, but none was so brutally efficient in the slaughter of human beings as were the Nazis. It has been plausibly argued that the cold-blooded efficiency of the Nazis was a direct result of their employing modern instrumental reason.[27] Such reason is everywhere in evidence, from the "rationalized" structure of the Nazi bureaucracy to the use of the latest modern technology in the design of the gas chambers at the Nazi death camps.

Nor can we afford to overlook those problematic consequences of science and technology that threaten us at the present moment. The preeminent examples here are undoubtedly the destruction of the natural environment and the possibility of the nuclear annihilation of the human species. While threats of this sort are surely not the inevitable consequences of modern calculative reason, technical, calculative reason possesses no built-in safeguards against such threats.

In addition to calling our attention to the consequences of modern technical reason, postmodern critics charge that moderns were deceived about the very nature of that reason. Natural science provides a clear example. Modernity exalted natural science as a paradigm of secure knowledge, a way of knowing that is totally objective, independent of the perspectives of the individuals who use it or the societies in which it is employed. But are the procedures for verifying or falsifying scientific theories really as objective and as straightforward as they initially seem? One of the most familiar ways to test a scientific hypothesis is to determine what observable events should occur according to the hypothesis and what sorts of events would contradict the hypothesis, and then to check and see how the hypothesis squares with the actually observed facts. If the facts contradict the hypothesis, it is falsified. If, in a large number of instances, the facts are as the hypothesis predicted, the hypothesis has empirical support.

The post-modern critic raises questions such as these: first, is it really so obvious that the ability to predict observable phenomena is equivalent to knowledge? Who is to say that the ability to predict the behavior of the world around us is equivalent to *knowing* that world? What is the basis for this assumption, an assumption built into the calculative method of scientific thinking?

Second, isn't there an element of circularity in the notion that observed events can help to verify or falsify a theory, inasmuch as the observation of those events may very well take place within the context of the very same theory? There is no such thing as a "pure" observation, one that is not interpreted by its observer. Instead, the observation becomes an observation only as it is placed within the context of an interpretive framework.

Quite apart from these first two difficulties, what does the scientist do when he or she is faced with two competing theories, each of which is equally accurate at predicting observable phenomena and neither of which can be conclusively falsified? He or she may favor the one that has more explanatory power, i.e., the theory that can provide a more complete and convincing account of the data at hand. Or perhaps the nod will be given to the theory that is simpler, the one that explains the data more economically. But surely decisions of this sort are not purely objective. How is one to determine which theory is simpler or has more explanatory power? Circularity is again a factor, insofar as the criteria will tend to arise from within the particular theories themselves: from the perspective of theory "a," theory "a" will surely seem to have more explanatory power. Or the decision will be a function of the personal preferences of the scientist. For instance, the criteria of simplicity will be drawn from the aesthetic inclinations of the investigator. Thus, we find scientists favoring the theories that they deem more "elegant." In addition, there is no objective way to weight these various factors. That is, scientists cannot quantify things like simplicity. They are not in a position to say, for instance, that while explanatory power is worth 10 points in gauging the strengths of a particular theory, simplicity is worth 5 points.

A word of caution is in order when evaluating this kind of critique of science: the critique does not imply that the scientific method is invalid as a way of knowing. Rather, it simply calls into question some of the naive assumptions entertained in modernity about this way of knowing. We now recognize, says the postmodern critic, that while the scientific approach to the world can indeed provide us with knowledge, science is more complicated and more dependent upon the relative perspectives of those who employ it than modernity recognized.

Where does all of this leave theology? The theologian might be tempted to use the critique of science outlined above as an escape hatch. He or she might reason this way: natural science is the paradigm of knowledge in modern society, and this has created difficulties for theology insofar as theology has been expected to justify its way of thinking according to the standards exemplified by science. But now we see that science is not the absolutely secure, totally objective avenue to knowledge that moderns supposed it to be. Thus, theology no longer needs to defend itself. Theology can now go its way undisturbed, advancing whatever claims to knowledge that it wishes.

Any such reading of the contemporary situation is, however, mere illusion. The fact that the postmodern mentality evaluates science differently from the modern in no way entails the conclusion that, for postmodern thinkers, all ways of thinking are now valid and hence exempt from the need to defend their claims to knowledge. The postmodern man or woman, to the same degree as the modern, will demand that theology observe the principle of universal accountability and will quite properly remain skeptical of theology's claim to know the infinite until theology has defended that claim.[28] The postmodern mindset is suspicious not simply of how science has perceived itself in modernity but of the general human tendency to deceive oneself where claims to knowledge are concerned. Indeed, the devastating critiques of theism mounted by thinkers like

Feuerbach, Marx, and Freud are not modern but characteristically postmodern in their attempt to find the unconscious motivations and subterranean sources of theistic belief (though it is interesting to note that both Marx and Freud took pains to show that their own methods were at least analogous to that of natural science and that Feuerbach's philosophy ended in a crass version of materialism, according to which all phenomena can be reduced to functions of matter). Furthermore, the postmodern world is every bit as secular as the modern. There are as many postmodern persons as there are modern for whom a church or a synagogue is a puzzling relic from a time long past, a place that is now a haven more for superstition than for genuine belief:

"But superstition, like belief, must die,
And what remains when disbelief has gone?
Grass, weedy pavement, brambles, buttress, sky,
A shape less recognizable each week,
A purpose more obscure."[29]

And insofar as secularization brings pluralism in its wake, the pluralism that challenged modern religion and theology will challenge their postmodern counterparts as well.

Nonetheless, the shift from a modern to a postmodern perspective does change things for theology. Theology must still address the external demand for universal accountability and the external skepticism about knowing the infinite, but it is no longer the case, as it was in modernity, that the method of the natural sciences is considered the paradigm of knowing if not the sole avenue to genuine knowledge. Recall, for example, Martin Heidegger's contention, mentioned in Chapter One, that the way of thinking that allows us to think Being cannot be the instrumental, calculative sort of thinking found in the natural sciences but must be something wholly different. To the extent that the postmodern mind acknowledges the possibility of other ways of knowing in addition to that represented by science, theology's claims, while they must be defended, are not ruled out in advance.

Our investigation of the modern and postmodern environments has uncovered the roots of the external forms of the demand for universal accountability and the skepticism about the possibility of knowing the infinite. When this is coupled with our intratheological investigation from Chapter One, it is apparent that the theologian must advance his or her theological position with the greatest of care. His or her theology will have to be carried out within the general framework provided by our tripartite *logos* formula, the implications of which are summed up in the notion of correlation.

Now, this framework is very general indeed, and it would be helpful to have the obligatory characteristics of theological inquiry worked out in much finer detail. This would only be possible, however, if there were agreement among theologians about the specifics of the *how* of theological knowing. But there is, in fact, no such agreement. In an analysis of the different kinds of argument employed by contemporary theologians, David Kelsey notes that "there is no special theological 'way' to argue or 'think,' if that is taken to imply a peculiarly theological structure to argument. Accordingly, analysis and criticism of theological 'systems' are not likely to be illuminating if undertaken on the tacit assumption that they may be measured by an ideal or standard mode of 'theological thinking,' 'theological method,' or 'theological way of arguing.' "[30] Thus, while the nature of the subject matter of theology as well as the modern and postmodern environments require that we do adhere to the general notion of a correlative theology, to set forth a more exacting set of standards would be to render our inquiry idiosyncratic and to rule out in advance the inumerable theological positions that do not match those standards.

Our task in the next chapter, then, will be to examine a number of theologies with a view to discovering whether they meet the requirements of our tripartite *logos* formula and, if so, how they fill out that general formula. We are not going to dictate in advance the specifics of the *how* of theological knowing. Rather, we are going to let the different theologians display their particular approaches. And insofar as the *how* of theological knowing and its *what* are reciprocally related, it is reasonable to assume that the diversity of perspectives on the *how* that we shall examine in the next chapter will be matched by a multitude of perspectives on the *what*, a potential embarrassment of theological riches.

What Do We Know, and How Do We Know It?

The purpose of this chapter is to show how the criteria set forth in Chapters One and Two relate to actual theological positions. We shall discover, first of all, that our tripartite *logos* formula does indeed dictate that not all contemporary theological proposals can be accepted. This will become apparent in our investigation of the theology of Karl Barth.

Second, we shall find that there are many contemporary proposals that meet the requirements of our *logos* formula, and that these proposals are, at the same time, often very different from one another. They fill out the *how* of theological knowing, and thus also the *what*, in a multitude of ways. This should make it clear that contemporary theologians do not agree about the specifics of the *how* and the *what* of theological knowledge.

The positions to be explored in this chapter by no means exhaust the current theological scene. They are intended to provide useful examples, not a comprehensive survey. Some of the criteria used in their selection have just been indicated: Barth's theology was chosen as an example of a position that must be deemed unacceptable, and the others are useful not only in that they meet the demands of our formula but also because they are all quite different from one another and thus demonstrate the diversity of contemporary theology. But there are other criteria at work in addition to these.

For instance, all of the positions but one, that of Nāgārjuna, are contemporary, and Nāgārjuna is not approached directly but via a contemporary interpreter. We are interested in contemporary examples because the particular species of theology at issue in our investigation is one that arises out of the modern and postmodern environments.

Another criterion is diversity of background: Barth and Cone are Protestants; Rahner and Ruether are Roman Catholics; Soloveitchik, Rubenstein, and Levinas are Jews. Whitehead's theological perspective arises out of no particular religious tradition. And while our exploration is focused on Western theology, the selection of Nāgārjuna, who is a Buddhist, is intended to show that our formula for theology is applicable to non-Western perspectives as well.

Finally, all of the persons selected are, in my estimation, influential thinkers. Each has made or is making an impact on the world of theological thinking.

The logic behind the order in which the various thinkers will be considered is this: We shall begin with Karl Barth, who emphasizes the extraordinary otherness or transcendence of God and the resultant difficulty of attaining knowledge of God. Barth's response to this difficulty is to maintain that only those who make the leap of Christian faith can come to knowledge of the divine. We shall move next to Alfred North Whitehead, for Whitehead's thought provides a sharp and useful contrast to Barth's, since Whitehead relies solely upon universally available resources to construct his theological edifice; he makes no appeal to the unique resources of a particular religious tradition. Karl Rahner's theology will be next in line, for his is a position that can be interpreted as standing midway between the two extremes represented by the Barthian emphasis on Christian faith and the Whiteheadian preference for a purely philosophical perspective. With the thought of Joseph Soloveitchik, we shall make a transition to theological perspectives that emphasize a practical approach to the *how* of theological thinking, an approach that gives more attention to concrete problems of existence than to abstract arguments. It will become evident that this practical emphasis charactizes the thought of Cone, Ruether, Rubenstein, and Nāgārjuna, in addition to that of Soloveitchik. We shall conclude with Emmanuel Levinas, whose emphasis on the extraordinary transcendence of the divine will invite comparison with the theology of Karl Barth and, thus, lend an element of symmetry to our exploration.

Our procedure for exploring each position will be to begin with a brief account of the *what*, the particular notion of the infinite advanced by the thinker in question. This will include a consideration of the relationship of the infinite to the fundamental anxieties described by Paul Tillich. Then we shall discuss the *how* of theological knowledge (which will, of course, allow us to further specify the *what*). It is in this discussion of the *how* that the demand for universal accountability will prove to be especially important.

1. Karl Barth (1886-1968)

Any list of the most important Christian thinkers of the twentieth century would have to include the name of Karl Barth. Barth was a Swiss Calvinist, but his influence was felt throughout the Protestant world and, to a lesser degree, in non-Protestant Christianity as well. Pope Pius XII went so far as to call Karl Barth the most important dogmatic theologian since Thomas Aquinas, the great thirteenth century thinker who is often regarded as having set forth the definitive Roman Catholic theology (a dogmatic theologian is one who expounds the central teachings or dogmas of the Christian church).

What is the nature of the infinite to which Karl Barth attempts to point? Barth's version of *theos* is very much the personal God of the Christian tradition. This is the Trinitarian God, one divine being who is simultaneously Father, Son, and Holy Spirit. The second person of the Trinity, the Son, is believed to have taken on human form in Jesus of Nazareth who, consequently, is designated the Christ, the one "annointed" or chosen by God for a special task. Jesus the Christ dies on the cross in order to atone for the sin of the human race, thereby reestablishing harmony between God and his creation.

One of the distinctive features of Barth's account of the Christian God is his constant emphasis on God's radical transcendence. God is conceived as totally beyond the finite human realm. And while human beings are caught up in sin, God is by his very nature Goodness and Truth. As the early Barth puts it, God is "wholly other." Hence, we never encounter this God as an object at our disposal. Instead, God is always subject, i.e., the one who acts rather than that which is acted upon. God's radical transcendence of the finite world makes his incarnation in the man Jesus all the more remarkable.

It is clear that Barth sees God as an infinity that can deliver human beings from fundamental threats resulting from their finitude (though, as we shall discover later, it is not as clear that human beings are capable of knowing just when they have been delivered). Insofar as Barth focuses on God's gracious decision to enter into the human condition in Jesus and rescue humanity from sin, it is fair to say that the anxiety most centrally addressed by Barth's God is moral anxiety. But ontic anxiety and spiritual anxiety are also at issue. For instance, Barth echoes the traditional Christian claim that God raised Jesus from the dead and that this signals the possiblity of eternal life for all human beings. And he clearly holds that the life of Christian faith is supremely meaningful, for it puts the creature on the path intended by the Creator.

But just *how* does Barth come to know all of this? After all, if his God is radically transcendent, there must exist a gap between the being of God and the cognitive equipment possessed by human beings. Barth's answer to the *how* question always comes down to one word: revelation. Left to its own devices, the human mind is indeed impotent where knowledge of the divine is concerned, but in his grace, God decides to reveal himself to humanity, to disclose himself in his Word, which is the Christ.

God's revelation in Christ is worked out a bit differently in Barth's early theology from how it is conceived in his later thought. The most important publication of the early Barth is his commentary on one of the central documents contained in the Christian Scriptures, the apostle Paul's letter to the first-century Christian community in Rome. The first edition of Barth's *Romans* appeared in 1919, the second edition in 1922, and the work seized the attention of the Christian theological world. Here Barth explains that human beings can know God only through God's revelation of himself. While the Christian Bible does have a central role to play in theology, the Bible is not itself God's revelation. Rather, the purely human words of the Bible attest to the event of revelation, which is the life, death, and resurrection of Jesus Christ.

For the early Barth, God's transcendence of the finite world is so total that little more than the contradiction between his goodness and human sin is actually disclosed by his self-revelation in Christ. Here is one of the best-known statements from Barth's *Romans*: ". . . if I have a system, it is limited to a recognition of what Kierkegaard called the 'infinite qualitative distinction' between time and eternity, and to my regarding this as possessing negative as well as positive significance: 'God is in heaven, and thou art on earth.' The relation between such a God and such a man, and the relation between such a man and such a God, is for me the theme of the Bible and the essence of philosophy. Philosophers name this KRISIS of human perception— the Prime Cause: the Bible beholds at the same cross- roads—the figure of Jesus Christ."[31] The word *"krisis,"* from which the English "crisis" derives, is Greek. Among its possible meanings is judgment. God's self- revelation in Jesus Christ represents a crisis for human- ity's understanding of itself and its world; it is a judgment upon that understanding.

The early Barth is sufficiently concerned about pre- serving the infinite qualitative distinction between the divine and the human that he attempts to deny the possibility of any real interconnection of God and the finite world. Thus, in his description of the resurrection of Jesus we find Barth saying that "As Christ, Jesus is the plane which lies beyond our comprehension. The plane which is known to us, He intersects vertically, from above. . . . In the Resurrection the new world of the Holy Spirit touches the old world of the flesh, but touches it as a tangent touches a circle, that is, without touching it."[32] This skepticism about our ability to know the divine does not arise simply out of some kind of conservative piety, for Barth is very much aware of the external skepticism generated by modern and postmodern culture. As a matter of fact, Barth urges the Christian church "to outstrip even Kant in the careful preservation of the boundaries of humanity."[33] In any case, the church must recognize that there is no point of contact between the infinite God and finite human beings, no overlap between human nature and the divine.

But Barth later became disenchanted with this approach to God, for it turns out to involve a point of contact after all, a kind of negative interconnection. In the words of one of Barth's most reliable commentators, it is almost as if the early Barth is suggesting that theology can "start from the impossible situation of man and move to the reality of grace that makes all things possible."[34] The dilemma of human sin becomes a steppingstone to knowledge of God in that theologians can achieve knowledge of God by starting with the human condition and negating it; God is the reality wholly unlike sinful human being.

This takes us to the later Barth, a Barth who wants to make it clearer than he had in *Romans* that knowledge of God can come only from God, that one cannot move from human being to the divine, and who, at the same time, wants to be able to say much more about God than he was able to say in *Romans*. The major work to emerge from this period is the multivolume *Church Dogmatics*, which was still in progress when Barth died in 1968. The very title of the work suggests that Barth now thinks he can say more about God than simply that God stands in contradiction to human sin. Barth will attempt to derive the dogmas of the Christian church, with all of the information they purport to provide about God, from revelation. The later Barth would agree with other contemporary Christian thinkers that the event of God's revelation in Christ involves not simply the disclosure of information about the divine but God making *himself* present to human beings. Nonetheless, Barth now holds that information about God is entailed by his self-revelation and that, therefore, dogmatic theology is a real possibility.

Unlike *Romans*, the *Church Dogmatics* presents us with a significant, openly acknowledged "point of contact" between God's revelation and the human beings to whom it is addressed.[35] An analogy comes into play according to Barth: ". . .our possibility of knowing God's Word is the possibility of a clear and certain knowledge, not equal but at least similar to the clarity and certainty with which God knows Himself in His Word." This is not an ever present, static analogy, but one effected by God in the event of revelation or, more specifically, in that component of God's self-revelation in Christ which Barth calls the "event of faith."[36] Thus, it is an *analogia fidei*, an "analogy of faith."[37] That faith and, hence, the analogy of faith are effected by God means that, as Barth never tires of repeating, "the possibility of faith as it is given to man in the reality of faith can be understood only as one that is loaned to man by God. . . ."[38]

But what precisely is God doing when he effects the analogy of faith? Barth explains it this way: "Our concepts and words cannot claim that God is truly their object. But he can lay claim to our concepts and words; he can claim to be their true object. In doing this, he is not abolishing his truth or setting up a double set of truths; he is merely acknowledging *himself* in our concepts and words."[39] That is, God can choose, and sometimes does in fact choose, to make our all-too-human words instruments of his self-manifestation. On the basis of the analogy of faith, we are able to know God, indeed, to know him well enough to be able to engage in dogmatic theology. And, using the analogy of faith as his starting point, the later Barth can move on to other sorts of analogies as well. We learn things about the earthly sphere of existence by looking to the reality of God. For example, we can, says Barth, gain new insight into how human beings are meant to interact with one another by considering the interrelationships among the three persons of the Trinity. But note that here too, as with the analogy of faith, the movement is from God to the human: we don't understand God as a being analogous to ourselves, but ourselves as beings analogous to God.

Can Barth provide a concrete example of the analogy of faith? Can he point to a particular instance of human words being taken up by God in such a way that God actually becomes their object? Barth believes that an example is to be found in the work of the eleventh century Christian theologian Anselm of Canterbury. In his *Proslogion*, Anselm provides a formula which he thinks will allow Christians to understand that God exists, indeed that he must exist, a truth which they have hitherto accepted on the basis of faith but have not fully comprehended. Anselm describes his project, then, as *fides quaerens intellectum*, faith seeking understanding. He tells us that, in answer to a prayer, a special name of God was revealed to him, a name consistent with the notion of God embraced in Christian faith. God is to be understood as "that than which nothing greater can be conceived." This is not a definition of God, but a name that guides us in our attempts to understand him, a rule to which our thinking must adhere.

Note where this name leads our thinking about God. God is that than which nothing greater can be conceived. But surely it is greater to exist than not to exist. Therefore, we conclude that God exists. But we have to go further than this, for it is not enough simply to understand that God does in fact exist. The name "that than which nothing greater can be conceived" demands that we recognize that God must exist, that he exists necessarily. Which is greater, something that, while we do conceive of it as presently existing, can be conceived of as not existing, or something which we cannot conceive of as not existing? Obviously the latter is greater. Thus, God exists necessarily, he cannot be conceived of as not existing.

Here is how Barth evaluates Anselm's project: "Everything depends not only on the fact that God grants him grace to think correctly about him, but also on the fact that God himself comes within his system as the object of this thinking, that he 'shows' himself to the thinker and in so doing modifies 'correct' thinking to an *intelligere esse in re*," to an understanding of what exists, not simply in the mind, but in reality.[40] In other words, God provides the ability to know, and he himself becomes the object of knowledge, showing himself within Anselm's formula.

While Anselm claims that his formula is a revealed name of God, it obviously consists of ordinary human words. But in this formula, we have an example of how God can utilize merely human words in such a way that he becomes the object of these words. Now, the words "that than which nothing greater can be conceived" do not prove to the unbeliever that God must exist, for the unbeliever can always retort that we cannot move from mere thought to reality. *If* there were a being such that nothing greater could be conceived, *then* it would be true to say of that being that he must exist. But Anselm intends his formula to be employed within the context of the faith of the Christian church, i.e., by Christians who already believe that God exists and want to attain an understanding of his existence. Hence, in Barth's words, "It is a question of the proof of faith by faith which was already established in itself without proof."[41] And in the context of faith, God uses the name "that than which nothing greater can be conceived" to reveal himself. For through that formula, God can bring human rationality into harmony with the inherent rationality of his own being. The evidence that God effects this harmony is that the Anselmian formula guides the believer's thinking in such a way that the believer cannot conceive of God as not existing. There is produced a necessity in thought which mirrors or corresponds to the actual necessity of God's existence.

Suppose that, for the sake of argument, we were to grant to Barth that the Anselmian formula demonstrates the *possibility* of God making himself the object of human words, the possibility of the analogy of faith. We would still want to ask how one can know in any particular instance, other than that of the Anselmian formula itself, that God is in fact effecting an analogy of faith. For instance, how can we know that God uses as a medium for his self-revelation the words in the Christian Bible that describe Jesus and his message?[42] Barth answers that we cannot stand outside the event of revelation and judge, on the basis of criteria derived from human reason, that it is an event of revelation. Rather, the ability to know that something is a revelation is given by God as part of the revelation itself. It will be true, says Barth, that "God has spoken and man has heard. . . . It will be true in absolute independence of all the criteria of truth that the secular or even the religious man has first to provide and apply critically before he very kindly resolves to let what is true be true. . . . The possibility of knowledge of God's Word lies in God's Word and nowhere else."[43] Thus, when all is said and done, Barth's theology invites us to leap into what John Cobb has quite accurately labled the "closed circle of revelation."[44]

This brings us to our critique of Barth, for to say that in Barth's theology one can only leap into the closed circle of revelation means that, in the last analysis, Barth does not provde a sufficiently clear account of *how* he comes to know what he claims to know. Barth asserts that the God of Christianity exists but that there is no way for unaided human reason to know of his existence. Rather, God's existence and his nature are made known only through his self-revelation. But how do I know that something is a revelation? Don't I have to fall back on human reason when I make the judgment that event "x" is a revelation? No, says Barth, for the knowledge that it is a revelation is part of the revelation itself. This answer, of course, succeeds only in pushing the need to rely upon human reason back one step. It is akin to saying, "the knowledge that event 'x' is a revelation is itself a revelation." I must now ask how I know that the revelation that event "x" is a revelation is itself a revelation. In other words, we either find ourselves in what philosophers call an infinite regress or simply leap, without any independent intellectual justification, into the closed circle of alleged revelation. At least in a modern or postmodern world, this must be judged a violation of the rule that theologians have to explain just how they know what they claim to know.

But what about the fact, noted earlier, that Barth's God delivers human beings from the ontic, moral, and spiritual threats resulting from finitude? Doesn't this represent a correlation of the divine and the human and thus a foothold for genuine knowledge of God? Even here Barth wants to pull back from any suggestion of knowledge of God that is independent of revelation: "A new, regenerate man will arise. . . as the man whom God has addressed and who hears God, unknown, of course, to himself and others, in a newness that cannot be ascertained, for what can be ascertained in him will always be the old, not possessing himself, for to the extent that he possesses himself he certainly does not possess this regenerate man."[45] Even this avenue to theological knowledge is blocked.

The particular nature of Barth's violation of the demand that theologians explain the *how* of theological knowledge means that he has, at the same time, also violated the demand for universal accountability. Why? Because the leap into the closed circle of revelation is also the leap into the closed circle of Christian faith. One receives revelation only in the attitude of Christian faith. That is the way of being through which God effects an analogy between his Word and our merely human words. Barth would not have violated the principle of universal accountability if he had provided an external and universally available explanation of why it is at least plausible to regard Jesus of Nazareth as the incarnate Word of God (of course it is not clear that such an explanation is in fact possible). Then the decision to embrace the attitude of Christian faith, while finally still an existential matter beyond the scope of theology as an academic discipline, would have been shown to be a rational decision. Instead, Barth claims that one must adopt the attitude of Christian faith *before* one can know that Jesus is the Word of God and, thus, before one can participate in the analogy of faith. But this clearly violates the principle of universal accountability, for it means that one must be a member of the Christian community in order to know what Barth claims to know about God. Barth does not wish to hide from this implication of his theology. He proclaims, "We do not say: How can all men know the Word of God? or even: How can any man know the Word of God? We have already recalled that it is not an issue of men universally or of man in general but very concretely and specifically of man in the Church."[46] For ". . . the Church is the presupposition of knowledge of the Word of God."[47]

Of course, Barth would reply to our charge by claiming that we misunderstand the event of faith. It is not the case, he would say, that one first decides to engage in the act of Christian faith and is then in a position to grasp God's self-revelation in Christ. Rather,

Christian faith is a gift of God which God himself provides in the very act of self-revelation. This reply, however, does not advance the discussion in the least, for in order to see that it is correct one must make the very leap of faith that we are calling into question.

In summary, Barth views theology as "a wholly uninsured obedience" to the Word of God. He asserts that "the theologian has no proof to offer himself or anyone else that he is not being merely fanciful but hears and accepts God's word. He can only feel certain. He can give neither himself nor anyone else the comfort of legitimation proving that he is acting under *orders*. He can only *act* under orders and so bear witness to the presence of the command."[48] It turns out, then, that while Barth is constantly concerned to present a theology that ultimately derives not from human beings but only from God's own self-revelation, his refusal to offer any kind of external, universally available justification for his thinking means that he has ended up with a theology that is restricted not only to a purely human perspective but to a purely individual, subjective perspective. Wolfhart Pannenberg's conclusion appears inevitable: Barth's approach "is in fact the furthest extreme of subjectivism made into a theologial position. Whereas other attempts to give theology a foundation in human terms sought support from common arguments, Barth's apparently so lofty objectivity about God and God's word turns out to rest on no more than the irrational subjectivity of a venture of faith with no justification outside itself."[49] The untenability of Barth's theology, its subjectivism, becomes especially evident when one notes that persons from non-Christian religions could make claims about their faiths exactly parallel to the one Barth makes about his. In other words, the Muslim could claim that he or she knows Islam to be the true religion because that fact has been revealed by Allah, the Jew can say something similar about Judaism, and so on, until we have a whole set of competing claims with no criteria for adjudicating among them. In fact, Christians who hold beliefs different from Barth's may want to claim revelatory backing and enter the fray. There will be no way for the parties involved in this dispute to converse with one another about the validity of their claims. The victory will perhaps be awarded to the person who can shout the loudest.

Barth's theology is no model for the way of thinking that we seek. We will have to look elsewhere for a theology that meets the requirements outlined in our *logos* formula. Of course, this does not mean that there is no sense in which Barth can be regarded as a "theologian." There are at least two important senses in which he can quite legitimately be deemed a theologian: first, if one stands wholly within the circle of the Christian confession of faith and wishes to articulate a theological vision that makes no claims to apply outside that circle, then Barth's perspective will appear totally legitimate. In other words, while Barth cannot represent the kind of academic theology of central concern to us here, he can certainly represent the sort of purely "confessional" theology traditionally undertaken within the various religious confessions. Second, Barth's religious vision can even claim a place within the contemporary college and university: it is perfectly legitimate to study Barth's thought in the context of what is usually called the "history of theology." The historian approaches a particular theological perspective not in order to evaluate the adequacy with which it seeks to grasp the infinite, but as a cultural artifact. Thus, we must distinguish between the academic discipline known as the history of theology—here Barth's influential thought surely has a place—and the discipline known as constructive theology. The former reports upon and analyzes what theologians have thought, the latter is itself the very activity of theological thinking.

2. Alfred North Whitehead (1861-1947)

At present, the philosophy of Alfred North Whitehead exercises an extraordinary influence among theologians, especially in Christian circles. Whitehead's most important philosophical work and the prime source for our exposition of his worldview is *Process and Reality*, published in 1929. Proponents of the Whiteheadian perspective, which is called "process thought," hold that it provides a worldview that is fully consistent with contemporary science and that produces important insights into the being of the divine. For Whitehead, reality is best understood not in terms of static substances but in terms of an evolutionary creativity. Reality is ever in a process of becoming.

What kind of God inhabits this Whiteheadian universe? Whitehead embraces a species of *panentheism*. In opposition to classical Western *theism* (the perspective on God traditionally held by Jews, Christians, and Muslims), panentheism holds that God is not independent of the world; panentheists believe that the world affects the being of God. At the same time, panentheists claim that the being of God is more than simply the totality of the world. As the Greek roots of the word indicate—*pan* means all, and *en* means in—panentheism maintains that the world is included within the being of God.

Whitehead's version of panentheism suggests that God is dipolar, that is, that there are two fundamental poles to his being. The first pole, the primordial nature of God, is the ground of possibility, the source of the various options that can be actualized by entities in the world. This primordial nature, logically prior to the actually existing world, is infinite, unchanging, and unconscious.

Over against God's primordial nature there stands what Whitehead calls the consequent nature of God. The consequent pole is the being of God as it takes up and is affected by the actually existing world. In his consequent nature, God can "save" the world by combining its component events into a harmonious whole in which good triumphs over evil.[50] Because the world taken up into the consequent pole is always in a process of becoming, the consequent pole itself is always in process. Whitehead explains that it is finite: God's consequent nature can never be complete, since the becoming of the world is never complete. He goes on to argue that, while God's consequent nature is temporal (i.e., it exists within the changing world of time), it is also everlasting. Thus, even though the events that make up the world all must pass, they are provided a kind of immortality—Whitehead calls it "objective immortality"[51]—by being taken up into the everlasting consequent nature of God. Finally, Whitehead indicates that God's consequent nature is conscious.

Although Whitehead's evolving God is partially finite, this God is infinite in the sense required by our definition of *theos*: he is able to deliver human beings from fundamental threats connected with their finitude. For instance, Whitehead's God addresses moral anxiety insofar as his consequent nature effects the triumph of good over evil. To the extent that the possibilities provided every person, indeed every event, by God's primordial nature are construed as values, the primordial nature too is relevant to moral anxiety. The anxiety of death can presumably be conquered through a recognition of objective immortality. And one can hardly suffer the emptiness and meaninglessness signified by spiritual anxiety if one recognizes that one always lives in relation to the Whiteheadian deity, for that deity is the primary instrument of the "creative advance into novelty," the evolving process that is the "ultimate metaphysical ground" of reality.[52]

Even from this very brief introduction to Whitehead's theological perspective, it should be clear that he offers an elaborate vision of the divine. How does he claim to know all of this? Unlike Barth, Whitehead makes no appeals to revelation, nor does he claim that one must make a faith commitment to a religious tradition. Instead, he relies solely upon the ability of human reason to grasp the nature of reality. He draws upon that reason to engage in what he terms "descriptive generalization."[53] In other words, Whitehead attempts to describe the most general features of reality, those fundamental features possessed by all instances of what is real.

Whitehead is aware that any such descriptive undertaking will be powerfully affected by the vantage point from which one views the reality to be described. Thus, he specifies the particular vantage point that, in his estimation, is the most rational one to occupy: we are urged to embrace the "reformed subjectivist principle." He explains that "the subjectivist principle is that the whole universe consists of elements disclosed in the analysis of the experiences of subjects."[54] Put generally, the subjectivist principle means that reality is best understood by focusing on how we as subjects experience reality, rather than by abstracting from our subjectivity in the mistaken assumption that it is irrelevant to underthanding the reality outside ourselves. This general version of the subjectivist principle can be worked out in a number of different ways. We have seen one example in the critical philosophy of Immanuel Kant. Recall the nature of Kant's transcendental exploration of knowledge: he looked for the conditions of the possibility of knowledge within the human subject, and he concluded that the only genuine knowledge we possess is knowledge of how things appear to the experiencing subject; our subjectivity conditions the knowing process and, as a result, we can never grasp reality as it is in itself. Thus, we might call Kant's philosophy a skeptical product of the subjectivist principle.

But Whitehead's *reformed* version of the subjectivist principle does not lead to a Kantian skepticism. Whitehead's approach to the *how* of philosophical and theological knowledge involves a thorough familiarity with and rejection of Kant's analysis. He goes so far as to say that his own position is "the inversion of Kant's philosophy."[55] When Whitehead says that the whole universe consists of elements disclosed in a description of the experience of subjects, he means that the reality outside the experiencing human subject actually has subjective characteristics of its own. In fact, everything that exists is ultimately composed of entities that have the character of subjects and are rudimentary instances of "experience." Whitehead calls them "actual entities": " 'Actual entities'—also termed 'actual occasions'—are the final real things of which the world is made up. There is no going behind actual entities to find anything more real. . . . these actual entities are drops of experience, complex and interdependent."[56] The objects that we encounter in the world around us such as stones and chairs and human beings are structures made up of countless actual entities. Because actual entities are drops of experience, they are to be understood as analogous to our own subjectivity.

If the "experience" attributed to actual entities were equated with *conscious* experience, then Whiteheads's position would be ludicrous. But he has in mind a much simpler and more basic type of experience, a fundamental experiential capacity that, while it a prerequisite for consciousness, can never be equated with that much more complex phenomenon. Actual entities are subjects that experience insofar as they are able to create themselves by freely drawing upon the possibilities and actualities in the reality round about them. As such, they are not mere objects acted upon but themselves actors, subjects for which other things are objects. Consistent with Whitehead's emphasis on process, these actual entities are radically temporal (thus, the term "actual *occasion*" may be preferable to "actual entity"). They exist but for a moment and then become objects for newly emerging subjects. Reality as a whole is an evolving process precisely because it is composed of series of constantly emerging and perishing actual occasions.

How, exactly, do actual occasions draw upon *possibilities* and *actualities* in the reality round about them? The pure *possibilites*, not now realized but always capable of realization in some actual occasion, Whitehead calls "eternal objects."[57] The eternal objects are, in John Cobb's phrase, "forms, relations, or qualities in abstraction from any particular embodiment."[58] The *actualities* which actual occasions can draw upon are those options that have already been realized by previous actual occasions. Thus, an actual occasion freely creates itself using the materials derived from eternal objects and other actual occasions. Now, an actual occasion cannot choose the particular eternal objects that it will draw upon, and when this is coupled with the fact that the actualities from which it can draw are limited in number, it becomes apparent that the freedom involved in the creation of an actual occasion is limited, not absolute. But freedom is involved nonetheless, for the occasion is free to "decide" how it will utilize the possibilities and actualities at its disposal. In summary, then, actual occasions, the drops of experience that make up the universe, are dipolar: they create themselves by drawing upon two basic sources, viz., eternal objects and previous actual occasions.

We are now in a position to grasp the *how* of theological knowledge. Whitehead's method of descriptive generalization seeks to uncover those basic characteristics that apply to all that is. Thus, if he is to be consistent, Whitehead will have to apply the results of his investigation even to his discussion of God. In an oft-quoted statement from *Process and Reality*, Whitehead asserts, ". . . God is not to be treated as an exception to all metaphysical principles, invoked to save their collapse. He is their chief exemplification."[59] Because we have seen that actual occasions are dipolar, we are not surprised to find Whitehead concluding, only a few pages later, "Thus, analogously to all actual entities, the nature of God is dipolar. He has a primordial nature and a consequent nature."[60] The primordial nature of God is his grasp of the whole realm of eternal objects. The consequent nature of God is his grasp of the whole world of actual occasions.

That Whitehead describes God as an actual occasion that shares, at least analogously, the properties common to all actual occasions indicates that he takes very seriously the need to correlate the divine and the human. We cannot expect to know anything about God if he is totally independent of the finite world of which we are a part, and Whitehead criticizes what is often taken to be the traditional Judeo-Christian concept of God precisely insofar as it suggests that God is such an independent entity. In a set of lectures published in 1926 under the title *Religion in the Making,* Whitehead complains that what he calls the "Semitic" concept of God "leaves God completely outside metaphysical rationalization. We know, according to it, that He is such a being as to design and create this universe, and there our knowledge stops." He goes on to explain, "Any proof which commences with the consideration of the character of the actual world [the only genuinely possible kind of proof in Whitehead's estimation] cannot rise above the actuality of this world. It can only discover all the factors disclosed in the world as experienced. In other words, it may discover an immanent God, but not a God wholly transcendent. The difficulty can be put in this way: by considering the world we can find all the factors required by the total metaphysical situation; but we cannot discover anything not included in this totality of actual fact, and yet explanatory of it."[61] God can only be known if he can be brought into correlation with the world in which we exist, and Whitehead's God can easily be correlated with the world since it is a part of his being. Or, as an alternative formulation, God and the world are both contained in a larger whole, the total metaphysical situation, the ongoing creative process.

Of course Whitehead must still supply further information about how he knows what he claims to know about God. For thus far all that we have actually determined is that Whitehead's description of God is consistent with his pronouncements about the general character of reality and that he correlates his God with the world of human experience. But how do we know that this God in fact exists? Whitehead must show not only that his God is consistent with the results of descriptive generalization about reality, but also that such a God is somehow demanded by descriptive generalization. This he attempts to do by arguing that "apart from the intervention of God, there could be nothing new in the world, and no order in the world."[62] Novelty and order can only be explained by reference to the Whiteheadian God.

If actual occasions could draw only upon other actual occasions, there would be no novelty in the world, for the options that have already been actualized would be the only options available. Novelty requires that actual occasions be able to draw also upon pure possibilities, options not actualized by any previous occasion, i.e., the eternal objects. But precisely insofar as they are pure, nonactual possibilities, the eternal objects are cut off from the world of actuality and hence ineffective there.

53

The primordial nature of God, which envisages all of the eternal objects, is required as a mediating factor to introduce the eternal objects into the actual world. In other words, without God the actual occasions would have no access to the realm of eternal objects.

What is more, there must be some limiting principle that makes for the harmony of the world by seeing to it that each actual occasion draws upon just those eternal objects that will be consistent with the options actualized by every other occasion. If the freedom of actual occasions were not bounded by this principle of limitation, the world would not be a world, but only chaos. It is God who provides the limiting principle.

God is required, then, to assure both the orderliness of the world and the novelty of the world. Both requirements are met by his primordial nature. And if we think back to the early part of our discussion of Whitehead's God where it was pointed out that God's consequent nature takes up the actual world into his being and effects the triumph of the good, we can add that God is also required if good is to conquer evil. Of course this third requirement is weaker than the first two: *if* good triumphs over evil, then this God must exist. But it is not clear that good does in fact conquer evil. By contrast, it is quite clear that the world exhibits order and novelty, and, on Whitehead's terms, this entails that God exists.

Alfred North Whitehead's account of God meets the demands of our *logos* formula. Whitehead engages in a process of descriptive generalization about reality that can in principle be grasped and evaluated by all intelligent human beings. There is no suggestion that one must make a leap of faith or succumb to the authority of a particular religious tradition. He sets forth clearly exactly *what* he thinks God is like and precisely *how* he comes to know what God is like. Whitehead's theology is fully correlative in the sense set forth in Chapter One. Of course, none of this suggests that we are compelled to agree with Whitehead. Adherence to our *logos* formula by no means assures that a position is true, but only that it is a candidate that ought to be taken seriously! There are obvious questions that would have to be explored before one could pronounce upon the final worth of Whitehead's philosophy: is Whitehead's use of the method of descriptive generalization sound? What about the reformed subjectivist principle? And even if one accepts the method of descriptive generalization and the reformed subjectivist principle, does the resultant worldview really require the existence of God, or could novelty and order be better explained in some other, simpler fashion? Such questions become all the more pressing when we discover that other thinkers propose very different theologies and yet seem to adhere just as successfully as does Whitehead to the demands of our *logos* formula.

3. Karl Rahner (1904-1984)

Karl Rahner, probably the most influential Roman Catholic theologian of the twentieth century, sets forth a theological position that, in many ways, stands between the Barthian and Whiteheadian approaches to God. This holds for both the *what* and the *how* of theological knowledge.

We begin with the *what*. On the one hand, Rahner's notion of the divine, like Barth's and unlike Whitehead's, is solidly situated within the context of orthodox Christian pronouncements about God. Rahner seems to be concerned to preserve the changelessness of God; his God is, in some sense at least, "immutable."[63] And rather than having always had the world as an integral part of his nature, this God freely created the world out of nothing. He is the Trinitarian God, Father, Son, and Holy Spirit. The second person of this Trinity became incarnate in the man Jesus of Nazareth and, in that form, provides the definitive revelation of God to man and woman. Thus, Rahner's God can be expected to address the three fundamental anxieties in basically the same fashion as the Christian God has always been conceived to do so, just as we saw that Barth's God did.

On the other hand, there is at the same time a panentheistic cast to Rahner's reflections: "*that* God really does not exist who operates and functions as an individual existent alongside of other existents, and who would thus as it were be a member of the larger household of all reality."[64] God and the world do not stand side by side. Rather, the world is a moment within the larger being of God, albeit a moment which need not have been, a moment that God freely chose to create.

An understanding of Rahner's version of panentheism

presupposes a grasp of his concept of the "real symbol." For Rahner, "all beings are by their nature symbolic, because they necessarily 'express' themselves in order to attain their own nature."[65] This is especially true for self-conscious beings, for self-consciousness rests upon a being expressing itself in something other than itself. How do human beings attain self-consiousness? They have to objectify themselves, i.e., place an expression of the self outside the self so that the self becomes an object, something that one can reflect upon. Human beings must express or symbolize themselves to themselves. Something similar goes on, says Rahner, in the preeminent instance of self-consciousness: God is self-conscious insofar as God the Father expresses himself in God the Son, who is also known as the "Word" precisely because he is the expression of God. The Trinity is the primal instance of real symbolism, in which a being moves outside itself, thereby expressing itself and attaining its true nature.

God's creation of the world and human life is a continuation of this movement in which God expresses himself in his other. But whereas the Trinitarian movement of self-expression is an integral, necessary element of God's nature, his creation of the world and humanity is something in which he freely chooses to engage. Nonetheless, if creation is a matter of God expressing himself in his other, it is evident that creation is a moment within the being of God, a fact clearly announced in Rahner's assertion that "when God wants to be what is not God, man comes to be."[66] Not surprisingly, Rahner holds that the perfect and complete instantiation of God in his created other is to be found in the incarnation of the second person of the Trinity, the Son or Word, in the man Jesus. When we look at the incarnate Son, we discover that Rahner's God, while in one sense immutable, is at the same time mutable: ". . . the God who is not subject to change in himself can change in something else, can become man. . . . The mystery of the Incarnation must be in God himself, and precisely in the fact that, although he is immutable in and of himself, he *himself* can become something in another."[67] Thus, even Jesus' death on the cross must be understood as a moment within the being of God. Rahner refers to it as the "death *of God* in his being and in his becoming in the other of the world."[68] It is surely evident, then, that while Rahner rejects certain forms of panentheism—e.g.,he wants to avoid the kind of panentheism developed by the nineteenth century German philosopher G.W.F. Hegel—he has developed his own unique version of Christian panentheism.[69] Rahner's God stands between the deities described by Barth and Whitehead in that his God is the Christian Trinity, immutable in and of himself, yet a God who genuinely changes in his created other and who contains the world panentheistically within his own divine being.

The *how* of theological knowledge as construed by Rahner also stands somewhere between the versions set forth by Barth and Whitehead. On the one hand, Rahner maintains that the central truths of the Christian tradition can be fully grasped only when one gives oneself over to them in an attitude of faith: "Faith. . . can reach that by which it is grounded and borne [i.e., the divine reality] only in. . . the act of faith itself."[70] This is so, explains Rahner, because "a question which by its very nature challenges and confronts the whole of human existence cannot be posed to begin with as a question for which particular elements of the concrete existence of the subject doing the asking can be put in parentheses."[71] In other words, as our juxtaposition of *theos* with ontic, moral, and spiritual anxiety indicates, the issues invovlved in the question about *theos* have to do with the essence of human being and hence with all dimensions of that being. Thus, if only the cognitive dimension is engaged, one cannot possibly grasp the question at issue in its entirety. A hypothesis about *theos* can only be tested, as it were, by attempting to live out the implications of the hypothesis, i.e., by engaging not only one's cognitive capacity but one's will and emotions as well. And, speaking practically, to truly live out the implications of the hypothesis is to already accept its truth. Thus, there is an element of circularity in the Christian approach to knowledge of God; Christian faith is circular.

But Rahner is not a Barthian. He goes on to explain that, despite the element of circularity in faith, "this neither excludes nor declares superfluous the process by which . . . [the Christian] can and must justify his experience before the tribunal of conscience and of truth."[72] Again, the fact that what is sought "is given only in faith itself, does not eliminate the possibility of articulating the grounds of faith to nonbelievers."[73] What Rahner seems to be suggesting is that, while Christian faith is circular, this fact does not eliminate the possibility of examining the Christian God via what we are calling theology as a way of thinking. Such a theology cannot grasp all that Christians claim is

graspable in the attitude of Christian faith, but, contrary
to what Barth would say, this theology can definitely
grasp a good deal about the Christian God. This is so
for at least two reasons.

First, Rahner suggests that there is an initial, external
plausibility to Christian faith. Christian faith is not
wholly circular. One does not simply leap into it without
any rational basis for doing so. We shall discover, for
instance, that acknowledging the reality of God is not an
intrafaith undertaking to the same degree as is acknowledging that Jesus is the incarnation of God. It should be
possible, then, for a discipline that stands outside of
Christian faith to grasp this external plausibility. As
external, it is universally available.

Second—and here we come upon an intriguing possibility for relating theology as a way of thinking to the
various religious traditions—someone like Rahner who
claims to stand within the circle of Christian commitment can perhaps give rational, universally available
expression to some of what he has discovered by living
out the Christian hypothesis. Of course, part of what is
meant by saying that certain truths are available only via
faith is that these truths cannot ever be fully grasped
except by one who has engaged his or her whole being in
accepting them; thinking alone is not enough. But
another part of what is meant may be that one cannot
think certain truths correctly *until* one has tried them
out by putting them into practice in one's life. But after
one has done so, perhaps he or she can, at least to some
extent, articulate for others what he or she has discovered in the life of faith.

In any case, Rahner certainly does present rational
arguments on behalf of the plausibility of the Christian
notion of God, and our task is to come to an
understanding of what he has to say. What, for Rahner,
is the universally available component of the *how* of
theological knowledge? Like both Barth and Whitehead,
Rahner is thoroughly familiar with the philosophy of
Immanuel Kant and the challenge that it presents to
theological thinking. As a matter of fact, Rahner
employs the kind of "transcendental" analysis initiated
by Kant. His theology is a species of what has come to
be called "transcendental Thomism" because it utilizes
Kantian transcendental analysis in conjunction with the
basic theological worldview of Thomas Aquinas.

In agreement with other transcendental Thomists,
Rahner maintains that, while Kant's transcendental
approach is indeed useful, Kant himself misinterpreted

its results. According to Rahner, an examination of the conditions for the possibility of human knowledge results in the discovery that an unthematic knowledge of God is presupposed in all acts of knowing, even the most mundane. To say that this knowledge of God is unthematic means that it is not the sort of knowledge of which one is directly conscious or that one makes an explicit object for reflection. Rather, it is the horizon in which all thematic knowledge is situated, analogous to the way in which my visualization of objects always takes place within some larger visual horizon. God is absolute, infinite being, and "the question about being belongs necessarily to man's existence, because it is implicitly contained in everything man thinks or says . . . . Every statement is a statement about some being. Hence it occurs against the background of a previous, although unthematic knowledge of being in general."[74] In every act of knowing a particular, limited object there is implicit a pre-grasp or, in Rahner's own German, a *Vorgriff* of the unlimited being that is *theos*.

Let us consider a more specific example of just how this occurs (Rahner's analysis utilizes the technical description of knowing supplied by Thomas Aquinas, but we shall avoid the technical Thomistic portions). Suppose that I see an object that I correctly judge to be a tree. What is involved in my grasping that particular entity as a tree? I must apply the concept *tree* to the individual entity that I see. But to be able to use concepts correctly is to recognize that concepts are "universals," that is, they are not limited to any particular instance or entity. I understand, in other words, that the concept *tree* and the quality of *treeness* that it represents do not apply only to this one physical thing that I now see before me but that they apply to many other things that have the same characteristics, i.e., to many other trees. Indeed, I understand that the concept and the quality could, in principle, apply to any number of other things that have the same characteristics, to any number of other trees. Concepts or universals are by their very nature without any built-in limitations as to the possible number of instances that can fall under them. To use concepts is to presuppose this lack of limitation.

What do we discover if we undertake a transcendental analysis of our knowledge of objects or, more specifically, our use of concepts? What are the conditions for the possibility of our grasping that the concept *tree* is in and of itself unlimited, even though our actual experience of *treeness* is always an experience of one individual entity, or at the very least of a limited number of entities? Rahner answers that human knowing must be dynamic, it must be a continuous movement which always reaches out for more than the individual being that it grasps in any particular act of knowing. "This 'more' can only be the absolute range of all knowable objects as such. We shall call this 'reaching for more' the *Vorgriff* (anticipation, pre-apprehension). Human consciousness grasps its single object in a *Vorgriff* which reaches for the absolute range of all its possible objects."[75] That is, human consciousness must, as a condition for the possibility of knowing individual beings, reach out toward unlimited being.

But the *Vorgriff* grounds not only the possibility of knowing objects, it also grounds our freedom and our consciousness of ourselves: "it is only in the presence of the infinity of being. . . . that an existent is in a position and has a standpoint from out of which he can assume responsibility for himself."[76] The unlimited horizon of being provides the open space in which I can actualize my freedom and the vantage point from which I can look back upon the whole of my existence and thus become fully conscious of it.

As expected, Rahner goes on to identify the infinity of being at which the dynamism of human consciousness aims with the Christian God. We have seen that this infinity is the basis for our own being insofar as it grounds our self-consciousness, our freedom, and our knowledge of the world around us; it is what makes human being, in the fullest sense, possible. As such, it can properly be construed, says Rahner, as the loving Creator of the Christian tradition.

All of this allows Rahner to define man and woman as "spirit in the world," a phrase which serves as the title of the published version of Rahner's doctoral dissertation. What is the meaning of "spirit"? "Man is spirit, i.e., he lives his life while reaching unceasingly for the absolute, in openness towards God. And this openness towards God is not something which may happen or not happen to him once in awhile, as he pleases. It is the condition of the possibility of that which man is and has to be and always also is in his most humdrum daily life. Only that makes him into a man: that he is always already on the way to God, whether or not he knows it expressly, whether or not he wills it. He is forever the infinite openness of the finite for God."[77] But human being is not disembodied spirit. Rather it is the kind of spirit that is situated in a world. Here Rahner follows the example of his teacher, Martin Heidegger, whose name has already appeared several times in our discussion. Heidegger describes man and woman as "being-in-the-world."[78] For Rahner, to say that human being is spirit in the world is to say that man and woman do not know the infinite being of God directly, but via their knowledge of the entities that make up the world. We have an unthematic knowledge of God as the condition of the possibility of knowing the objects that confront us in our world. Perhaps in rare instances one can experience the infinite being of God without the mediation of worldly objects: "in mystical experience and perhaps in the experience of final loneliness in the face of death."[79] For the most part, however, our grasp of God is tied up with our grasp of the finite things round about us.

If all persons, just insofar as they are human beings, possess an unthematic knowledge of God as the presupposition of their every act of knowing and willing, it follows that human history, the arena in which this knowing and willing occurs, can be judged a continuous revelation of God to humankind. History is equivalent to *general revelation*, a revelation present to all persons in all times and places. Of course to refer to this process as general revelation does not change the fact that the knowledge of God that is imparted here is unthematic. We are not directly aware of the reality of God in all of our knowing and acting, and it may be that we go through life without ever making this unthematic revelation thematic. Our attention is always focused first of all upon knowledge about and action within the finite world, and we may never turn that attention to the conditions which make the knowledge and action possible.

What, then, about *special revelation*, the sort of revelation that goes beyond the general revelation that is given with the structure of human consciousness, the kind of revelation that is imparted in a particular time and place? Rahner defines special revelation this way: special revelation occurs where the interpretation "of God's transcendental self-communication in history succeeds, and where with certainty it reaches its self-awareness and its purity in such a way that it correctly knows itself to be guided and directed by God, and, protected by him against clinging tenaciously to what is provisional and to what is depraved, it discovers its own true self."[80] There may be certain instances, in other words, where God's continual revelation of himself is definitely made thematic and is given clear and correct articulation. The attempt at clear and correct thematic knowledge of God will succeed in spite of human ignorance and human malevolence.

While Rahner cannot conclusively demonstrate that Jesus the Christ is the definitive special revelation—here the circle of faith will undoubtedly come into play to some extent—he can at least offer some rational, universally available basis for the Christian's decision to embrace the faith that Jesus is such a revelation. For he can argue that in Jesus, God's self-revelation is grasped thematically and that, what is more, Jesus' presentation of God is uniquely clear and correct. Rahner argues that "in the genuine history of a dialogue in freedom between God and the human race, a point is conceivable at which God's self-communication to the world is indeed not yet concluded, but nevertheless the fact of this self-communication is already given unambiguously, and the success, the victory and the irreversibility of this process has become manifest in and in spite of this ongoing dialogue of freedom."[81] Here, then, are the criteria for determining if Jesus is in fact the definitive revelation of the divine.

If we now step back and evaluate Rahner's approach to theological knowledge, we must conclude that he does attempt to observe the principles represented in our *logos* formula. Though he is ever sensitive to the element of mystery in the being of God, Rahner does tell us a good deal about *what* his God is like, and via his transcendental analysis he tries to uncover a way of knowing God, a *how*, that is open to all persons given their very nature as human beings. We have noted that his ability to provide universally available grounds for the conviction that Jesus is the definititve revelation is open to more serious question than is his ability to provide such grounds for the general affirmation of the reality of God, but it is significant that he does at least offer some rational basis for Christology. We can read him as trying to indicate the initial plausibility of the Christian's claims about the Christ and to articulate in universally available terms what the Christian discovers in the life of faith.

Another way in which to indicate Rahner's basic adherence to our formula is to note that his theology is genuinely correlative. There is no question but that the divine touches and even enters into the human realm according to Rahner's panentheism. He even goes so far as to turn Feuerbach's critical dictum to theological advantage: ". . . all theology is eternally anthropology."[82] For in the incarnation of the eternal Word, God himself has become a human being, and it will remain the case for all eternity that human being is God in his otherness.

But, once again, Rahner's adherence to the principles of theology as a disciplined way of thinking does not guarantee the truth of his position. If we were to press on into an analysis of Rahner that would qualify us to pronounce on the final validity of his theology, we would have to raise questions not only about his Christology, but also about even more fundamental matters. For instance, does the unlimited horizon presupposed in all knowing and acting, assuming that it is in fact presupposed, really point toward the infinite being of some divinity? Or is this horizon perhaps only a property of consciousness, with no implications for what lies outside consciousness?

4. Joseph Soloveitchik (1903-   )

Orthodox Judaism may seem an unlikely source for theology as a way of thinking. The heart of Orthodoxy is strict adherence to the 613 commandments believed to have been revealed by God to Moses at Mt. Sinai. Thus, Orthodox intellectual inquiry tends to focus not on questions about the nature of the divine, but on the interpretation of the Halakhah, Jewish religious practice (often, and misleadingly, translated as "law") as it is contained in the Hebrew Bible, the Talmuds, and later rabbinic codes and commentaries. What is more, Orthodox Judaism is often regarded as a tradition with little interest in the larger culture and, hence, little inclination to adhere to the principle of universal accountability when engaging in religious reflection. But the thought of Joseph Soloveitchik, whom many regard as the leading intellectual figure in American Orthodoxy, is rich with possibilities for academic theology.

Now, there should be no confusion about the fact that Rabbi Soloveitchik is a man of faith. His primary concern is the community of practicing, Orthodox Jews, not the secular academy. But recall that in our discussion of Rahner, we recognized that a person of religious commitment might be able not only to articulate the initial plausibility of his or her act of faith, but also to give rational, universally available expression to what he or she discovers by living the life of faith. It is just such a possibility that confronts us in a work by Soloveitchik entitled *Halakhic Man*.[83]

Soloveitchik's God, the *what* of his theology, is the God who makes himself known not by revealing what he is like in and of himself but, rather, by revealing what he expects of his creatures. He is the God manifest in the Halakhah. It is through the Halakhah, then, that this God addresses ontic, moral, and spritual anxiety. The Halakhah deals with spiritual anxiety insofar as the commandments provide an all-encompassing framework for organizing one's life in a supremely meaningful fashion. Modern and postmodern meaninglessness are, to a large extent, the result of what sociologists call "anomie," the sense that the world is a chaos without organizing laws or principles. Thanks to the Halakhah, there is little experience of anomie for the Orthodox Jew. The Halakhah also provides an answer to moral anxiety, first of all in that it makes clear what kind of behavior is expected of human beings and, second, in that it allows for the possibility of repentance when one falls short of the commandments. Ontic anxiety may be addressed by trust in God's providence, which includes the belief that God will raise the righteous to a new life after death. But it is also addressed by the Halakhah's ability to create a life in the here and now that reflects the eternity of the divine. Yet again, the Halakhah tames the anxiety of death by fixing the phenomenon of death in rational categories, i.e., turning a hitherto unknown into an object of our cognition and thus defusing its terror.

How can we come to know that this God is real? This question is not of great concern to Soloveitchik, for he lives within the circle of Orthodox faith. He takes God's existence as a given. But perhaps his description of halakhic existence can be read as evidence of the validity of Orthodox Jewish belief. That is, instead of attempting to demonstrate the existence of the God of Abraham, Isaac, and Jacob directly, perhaps one can offer an in-depth description of life lived in accordance with the Halakhah and, by displaying its power, thereby give indirect testimony to the infinity said to be its source. If, for example, we are shown that halakhic existence can indeed address effectively the anxieties that manifest our finitude, will we not have to give some credence to the assertion that the Halakhah derives from the infinite being of the divine? This procedure would not entail a dispute with the Kantian claim that an infinite reality can never be given in sensible intuition. For it is a procedure that seeks not to grasp the infinite directly, but to find evidence of the infinite in the overturning of the dilemmas of finitude. In any case, we should not expect to find a quick and easy prescription for vanquishing anxiety in Soloveitchik's exposition of halakhic existence, for that existence arises out of struggle: "Out of the straits of inner oppositions and incongruities, spiritual doubts and uncertainties, out of the depths of a psyche rent with antinomies and contradictions, out of the bottomless pit of a soul that struggles with its own torments I have called, I have called unto Thee, O Lord."[84]

Halakhic Man, the Hebrew original of which was published in 1944, attempts a concise description of halakhic existence through the use of ideal types. Soloveitchik wants to present the clearest account possible of the halakhic life, but actual human beings seldom exhibit any way of being in its purity. Thus, he finds it useful to construct an ideal of halakhic existence, a model of what life would be like if constantly guided by the Halakhah, so that his readers can easily perceive the fundamental characteristics of halakhic man.

Of course, in order for Soloveitchik to construct this ideal, he must draw upon the fragmentary realization of halakhic existence in the lives of actual persons. Thus, his ideal types are based, indirectly, upon phenomenological description. Phenomenology is a philosophical method that seeks to uncover the essence of a particular thing by describing how it is originally given to human consciousness. In order to get at it in its pure form, the phenomenologist brackets or puts to one side the questions about and interpretations of the thing that subsequently arise. An example may be helpful here. Suppose that we wish to describe the essential characteristics of the object of a particular species of religious experience. A phenomenological analysis of that object will attempt to describe the nature of the object *as it appears in the religious experience*. We might be tempted to ask whether the object really exists outside the world of our experience or whether it is simply a product of the imagination, but that is the sort of question that must be bracketed. It is by bracketing such extrinsic matters that we are able to get to the essential core of the phenomenon, for this bracketing directs our attention to the object of religious consciousness *itself*.

Soloveitchik's procedure in *Halakhic Man* is to contrast the way of being he calls halakhic man with two other options, viz., *homo religiosus*, which is Latin for "religious man" and stands for a religious tendency that is apparently present in germ in all human beings, and cognitive man, who exhibits the realization of the rational capacity in human beings. Halakhic man takes up elements of both *homo religiosus* and cognitive man and combines them in a unique synthesis.

We start with cognitive man: "Cognitive man does not tolerate any obscurity, any oblique allusions and undeciphered secrets in existence. He desires to establish fixed principles, to create laws and judgments, to negate the unforeseen and the incomprehensible, to understand the wondrous and sudden in existence. Cognitive man establishes a cosmic order characterized by necessity and lawfulness."[85] Thus, cognitive man approaches the cosmos as something over which he can exercise dominion; cognition is a way of ordering and, ultimately, controling the world. Furthermore, cognitive man is concerned only with that which exists within the boundaries of time and space. The limitations that Kant put on knowledge seem self-evident to him.[86] For cognitive man, then, any talk about a divine reality beyond the finite world of which we are a part is out of the question.

Homo religiosus is a very different animal. As the opposite of cognitive man, he longs to be enveloped in mystery, specifically, the mystery of the divine. Soloveitchik describes him as a being shot through with conflict. Drawing upon Rudolf Otto's phenomenology of religious experience, Soloveitchik explains that *homo religiosus* feels at one and the same time an attraction to and an overwhelming fear of the divine.[87] Similarly, *homo religiosus* feels caught between loathing and admiration for his or her own being. Two verses from the book of Psalms in the Hebrew Bible testify to this duality: "When I behold Thy heavens, the work of Thy fingers, the moon and the stars which Thou hast established; what is man, that Thou art mindful of him, and the son of man, that Thou thinkest of him?" (Ps. 8:4-5) "Yet Thou hast made him but a little lower than the angels, and hast crowned him with glory and honor. Thou hast made him to have dominion over the works of Thy hands; Thou hast put all things under his feet" (Ps. 8:6-7).[88]

The contradictory character of the experience of *homo*

religiosus is summed up in the fact that he or she sees our existence in the physical world as a state of bondage from which we ought to desire escape; this world is in constant tension with a higher world. *Homo religiosus* wants to flee this world and be absorbed into the transcendent world of the divine. Here we must take note of Soloveitchik's severe criticisms of *homo religiosus*. First of all, "*Homo religiosus*, his glance fixed upon the higher realms, forgets all too frequently the lower realms and becomes ensnared in the sins of ethical inconsistency and hypocrisy. See what many religions have done to this world on account of their yearning to break through the bounds of concrete reality and escape to the sphere of eternity. They have been so intoxicated by their dreams of an exalted supernal existence that they have failed to hear the cries of 'them that dwell in houses of clay' (Job 4:19), the sighs of orphans, the groans of the destitute."[89] Second, this focus on a transcendent world tends to "constrict itself to a narrow, dark corner, relinquish the public domain, and give rise to a concept of religious esotericism." Hence, it produces "ecclesiastical tyranny, religious aristocracies, and charismatic personalities."[90]

Nor does Soloveitchik have any sympathy for *homo religiosus*' proclivity for mystery, emotion, and subjectivity: "The individual who frees himself from the rational principle and who casts off the yoke of objective thought will in the end turn destructive and lay waste the entire created order. Therefore, it is preferable that religion should ally itself with the forces of clear, logical cognition, as uniquely exemplified in the scientific method, even though at times the two might clash with one another, rather than pledge its troth to beclouded, mysterious ideologies that grope in the dark corners of existence, unaided by the shining light of objective knowledge, and believe that they have penetrated to the secret core of the world."[91] Soloveitchik finds this dangerous attitude in philosophers like Friedrich Nietzsche and Martin Heidegger, and he suggests that its fruits are evident in the world events occuring as he writes, i.e., in the 1940's.[92]

This brings us to halakhic man. As one might expect from what has just been said, halakhic man bears a strong resemblance to cognitive man. Halakhic man too is armed with laws with which the world can be structured; he employs a priori principles (principles that are prior to and independent of experience). According to Soloveitchik, "There is no phenomenon, entity, or object in this concrete world which the a priori Halakhah does not approach with its ideal standard." Here Soloveitchik provides an example that is most fascinating, precisely because it is so mundane and concrete: "When halakhic man comes across a spring bubbling quietly, he already possesses a fixed, a priori relationship with this real phenomenon."[93] That is, the Halakhah provides a readymade interpretation of the spring's legal and ritual significance: the spring is fit for a ritual of purification, the immersion of a man with a discharge; it may serve as waters of expiation—the Halkhah structures one's experience of the spring in these ways and more. It is so like the cognitive approach that it warrants a comparison with physics: "The Halakhah, which was given to us from Sinai, is the objectification of religion in clear and determinate forms, in precise and authoritative laws, and in definite principles. It translates subjectivity into objectivity, the amorphous flow of religious experience into a fixed pattern of lawfulness. To what may the matter be compared? To the physicist who transforms light and sound and all of the contents of our qualitative perceptions into quantitative relationships, mathematical functions, and objective fields of force."[94] The Halakhah is nothing if not rational.

But halakhic man is of course not just like cognitive man, for the Halakhah is, after all, given by God. The Halakhah puts one in touch with the transcendent. In short: "Halakhic man differs both from *homo religiosus*, who rebels against the rule of reality and seeks refuge in a supernal world, and from cognitive man, who does not encounter any transcendence. Halakhic man apprehends transcendence. However, instead of rising up to it, he tries to bring it down to him. Rather than raising the lower realms to the higher world, halakhic man brings down the higher realms to the lower world."[95] Soloveitchik fully develops the notion of bringing the divine into this world. He mentions the concept of the "contraction" of the divine infinity within the finite, a concept also mentioned in the Jewish mystical movement known as the Kabbalah. But there is a major difference here. The Kabbalists see the divine contraction as something to be remedied. They speak of it as the "Shekinah [divine presence] in exile," which should be reunited with the Godhead. But halakhic man views the contraction as wholly good and desirable. For it is the goal of halakhic man to bring the infinity of the divine into the finite world by actualizing the Halakhah.

It follows that there is even a certain superiority of this world over the next world, for "it is here that the Halakhah can be implemented. . . . It is here, in this world, that halakhic man acquires eternal life!" Soloveitchik quotes the rabbinic saying, "Better is one hour of Torah and *mitzvot* [commandments] in this world than the whole life of the world to come," and he claims that "this declaration is the watchword of the halakhist."[96] Human beings have a privilege that heavenly beings envy, the ability to actualize the Halakhah.

Such actualization wards off the anomie that causes meaninglessness. In fact, it allows man and woman to participate in God's creation of the world out of chaos. The notion that man and woman can be co-creators with God is "the central idea in the halakhic consciousness."[97] "The Creator, as it were, impaired reality in order that mortal man could repair its flaws and perfect it."[98] The privilege of being a partner of God in the act of creation applies not only to the macrocosm, but also to the microcosm: the human being must create *him-* or *herself.* Soloveitchik holds that "the contradiction that one finds in the macrocosm between ontic beauty and perfection and monstrous 'nothingness' also appears in the microcosm—in man—for the latter incorporates within himself the most perfect creation and the most unimaginable chaos and void, light and darkness, the abyss and the law, a coarse, turbid being and a clear, lucid existence, the beast and the image of God."[99] There is need for repair and creation in the inner world just as there is in the outer one, and the Halakhah gives man and woman the wherewithal to join in the creative work of God. Thus, it brings the infinite into the very midst of the finite, the eternal into the realm of the temporal: it is in this world that halakhic man and woman acquire eternal life. The Halakhah thus exercises dominion over ontic anxiety.

A central instance of creation of oneself is found in the act of repentance. Soloveitchik describes it this way: "The severing of one's psychic identity with one's previous 'I,' and the creation of a new 'I,' possessor of a new consciousness, a new heart and spirit, different desires, longings, goals—this is the meaning of that repentance compounded of regret over the past and resolve for the future."[100] Moral anxiety is checked. And just as halakhic existence taken as a whole is the synthesis of cognitve man and *homo religiosus,* so repentance as a particular aspect of halakhic existence overcomes the duality in *homo religiosus'* sense of the self as worthy both of approbation and condemnation.

How shall we evaluate all of this? Surely no theology could be more correlative than Soloveitchik's. He claims not just that there is a point of contact between the divine and the human, the infinite and the finite, but that the actualization of the Halakhah makes the divine present in the center of the finite world. Furthermore, the ability to make the divine present is not hidden in mystery, its secrets available only to an elite group of initiates. Rather, this ability rests in the commandments of the Halakhah, which are clear, rational, universally available precepts. What Soloveitchik has done, at least according to one possible interpretation, is to provide a phenomenological analysis of halakhic existence that exhibits the concrete power of that existence, its ability to unite the strengths of cognitive man and *homo religiosus* and to create an inner and an outer world that serve as the sanctuaries of the infinite.[101] We suggested at the outset how adherence to the Halakhah might address, if not vanquish, ontic, moral, and spritual anxiety. *Halakhic Man* can be read as attempting a phenomenological demonstration of the truth of that suggestion; its truth is not argued so much as made manifest by pointing to the concrete facts of halakhic existence. If halakhic existence does indeed provide a way beyond the fundamental anxities that derive from our finitude, then it offers genuine access to the infinite. The word "if" is, of course, all-important. Once again, the final validity of Soloveitchik's theology is something that we are not in a position to pronounce upon in this study.

5. *Liberation Theology: James Cone (1938-   ) and Rosemary Radford Ruether (1936-   )*

The designation "liberation theology" covers so many

diverse instances of theology that it is difficult to define just what it is. As Steve Gowler has observed, "Frequently, liberation theology is used as a generic term that covers such specific theologies as Latin American theology, feminist theology, Black theology, Asian theology, Native American theology, and others. Consequently, some maintain that it is more accurate and appropriate to use the plural and speak of theologies of liberation. This suggestion is well taken, although if followed too closely it might lead to a paralyzing scrupulosity that judges all general terms to be too imprecise." Gowler goes on to point out that there are in fact several significant characteristics which these various instances have in common: "In each case theological reflection is being done by persons who have traditionally found themselves politically, economically, and culturally on the margins of society, by persons who are using their newfound voices to speak out against the outrageousness of the world as they know it. The call for liberation from oppressive structures is theology because these formerly silent ones claim that the ground and pattern of their liberation can be found in the actions of the God who is witnessed to in the Bible."[102] Thus, following Gowler, I conclude that it is legitimate to employ the general designation "liberation theology."

We shall consider two North American instances of liberation theology: the black theology of James Cone and the feminist theology of Rosemary Radford Ruether. As always, we turn first to the *what*. Cone's God is, in the phrase used as a title for one of his books, the "God of the oppressed."[103] Cone is a Christian, and he reads the two testaments that make up the Christian scriptures as revealing a deity who sides with the powerless and poor and who acts to liberate them from their oppression. In the Old Testament we see, for instance, a God who frees the Hebrew slaves from Egypt and who thunders against oppressive social conditions through the mouths of his prophets. The New Testament shows the Christ, the incarnate Word of God, as the one who brings the good news of liberation to the outcasts and the poor. In that Christians identify the Christ not just with the historical individual Jesus of Nazareth but also as the Risen One who is present among Christians today, Cone asserts that "Jesus is black."[104] He acknowledges that this christological title may not be appropriate in every time and place. It must be noted, however, that "this was no less true of the New Testament titles, such as 'Son of God' and 'Son of David,' and of various descriptions of Jesus throughout the Christian tradition. But the validity of any christological title in any period of history is not decided by its universality but by this: whether in the particularity of its time it points to God's universal will to liberate particular oppressed people from inhumanity. This is exactly what blackness does in the contemporary social existence of America."[105] In this time and place, God identifies himself with black men and women, for they are the oppressed of this land.

What do we discover when we juxtapose Cone's God of the oppressed with Tillich's three fundamental anxieties? While the God of the oppressed can certainly address the three anxieties, it is likely that Cone would think our use of them as a key to the *what* of theological knowledge an errant procedure. The Tillichian anxieties are functions of the experience of the existing individual as an individual, not of the individual as a member of a social group. They are as relevant—Cone might say *more* relevant—to white middle class Europeans and Americans as they are to the oppressed of those societies. And, as we shall see when we discuss the *how* of theological knowledge below, Cone maintains that a perspective on God other than the one afforded by the concrete experience of oppression necessarily distorts one's theological vision.[106]

Be that as it may, Cone's God is by no means impotent in the face of ontic, moral, and spiritual anxiety. The God of the oppressed overcomes ontic anxiety, especially in the form of the "fate" of the oppressed, by breaking the power of the unjust forces that bind the oppressed to a destiny of suffering. God has done so in the past, he is doing so now, and he will do so decisively, once and for all, in the future. Cone keeps the eschatological element, the notion of the end-time when God will usher in his kingdom, in tension with the present: the oppressed look to the future as the locus of total liberation, but their resultant sense of hope empowers them to fight against injustice in the present. The same is true of the individual's hope for life after death in heaven: "Black people can struggle because they truly believe that one day they will be taken out of their misery."[107] The way in which the hope for eternal life has actually functioned in black American Christianity gives the lie to Marx's contention that such hope always serves as an opium that drugs the oppressed into submission.

The center of evil in the particular world of which we are a part is oppression. Thus, the pathway to overcoming moral anxiety is a genuine act of repentance, a radical conversion that involves abandoning one's ties to the structures that spawn racism and exploitation and alligning onself with those who take up the struggle against oppression.

The God of the oppressed conquers spiritual anxiety by showing the victims of oppression that they are his chosen ones. The victim knows "that he has an identity that cannot be taken away with guns and bullets."[108] One's sense of self-worth is placed on an eternal foundation.

The feminist theology of Rosemary Radford Ruether, though it arises out of the Christian worldview, is not as tightly bound as is Cone's theology to the tenets of traditional Christianity. The *what* of Ruether's theology is the reality she designates "God/ess," the "Primal Matrix" from which all things derive. God/ess is neither a god nor a goddess, but a reality that transcends stereotypical notions of "male attributes" and "female attributes." Ruether reasons that "if all language for God/ess is analogy, if taking a particular human image literally is idolatry, then male language for the divine must lose its privileged place. If God/ess is not the creator and validator of the existing hierarchical social order, but rather the one who liberates us from it, who opens up a new community of equals, then language about God/ess drawn from kingship and hierarchical power must lose its privileged place. Images of God/ess must include female roles and experiences. Images of God/ess must be drawn from the activities of peasants and working people, people at the bottom of society. Most of all, images of God/ess must be transformative, pointing us back to our authentic potential and forward to new redeemed possibilities. God/ess-language cannot validate roles of men or women in stereotypic ways that justify male dominance and female subordination."[109] Ruether understands this divine ground of being as encompassing not just women as well as men, the disadvantaged as well as the advantaged, but also matter as well as spirit, earth as well as heaven: "Here the divine is not 'up there' as abstracted ego, but beneath and around us as encompassing source of life and renewal of life; spirit and matter are not split hierarchically. That which is most basic, matter (mother, matrix), is also most powerfully imbued with the powers of life and spirit."[110]

While Ruether draws upon numerous religious traditions outside orthodox Christianity, she does regard

Jesus the Christ as a crucial figure. By giving women of marginalized groups a central role in his ministry, Jesus exhibited an iconoclastic messianism that demolishes the idolatry that is patriarchy. She concludes that, "theologically speaking, then, we might say that the maleness of Jesus has no ultimate significance. It has social symbolic significance in the framework of societies of patriarchal privilege. In this sense Jesus as the Christ, the representative of liberated humanity and the liberating Word of God, manifests the *kenosis* [self-emptying] *of patriarchy*, the announcement of the new humanity through a lifestyle that discards hierarchical caste privilege and speaks on behalf of the lowly."[111] What is more, Ruether would agree with Cone's contention that the Christ cannot be limited to the historical Jesus. She interprets the continuing reality of the Christ this way: ". . . Christic personhood continues in our sisters and brothers. In the language of early Christian prophetism, we can encounter Christ *in the form of our sister*. Christ, the liberated humanity, is not confined to a static perfection of one person two thousand years ago. Rather, redemptive humanity goes ahead of us, calling us to yet incompleted dimensions of human liberation."[112] At the same time, Ruether is suspicious of eschatology, for it tends to emphasize the future at the expense of the present and another reality at the expense of this one. We must abandon any attachment to the notion that a just order can be attained once-and-for-all; our finitude dictates that change will be a constant part of our experience, and the struggle for what is right a never-ending duty.

What of the Tillichian anxieties? Ruether would have us approach ontic anxiety by coming to accept our finitude, our proper place within the scheme of things: "Both change and death are good. They belong to the natural limits of life. We need to seek the life intended by God/ess for us within these limits."[113] As for personal immortality, a concept apparently of more concern to men than to women, Ruether suggests that the most realistic attitude is agnosticism. More important than personal survival of death is the opportunity to contribute something to the struggle for a just community.

Moral anxiety calls for conversion—recall Cone's similar position—the transformation of mindset that the Bible terms *metanoia*. According to Ruether, "Evil comes about precisely by the distortion of the self-other relationship into the good-evil, superior-inferior dualism.

The good potential of human nature then is to be sought primarily in conversion to relationality. This means a *metanoia*, or 'change of mind,' in which the dialectics of human existence are converted from opposites into mutual interdependence."[114] As a result, one receives the gift of community: community with other persons and community with nonhuman nature, which together manifest one's community with God/ess. And this brings us to spiritual anxiety, for surely such grounded-ness in the Primal Matrix and the human and nonhuman communities that rest upon it is equivalent to finding the source of all genuine human meaning.

It should be apparent by now that the *what* of liberation theology distinguishes it from other brands of theology. But the *how* of liberation thought turns out to be even more distinctive. Robert McAfee Brown has suggested that there are six characteristics of the *how* of liberation theology that distinguish it from more tradi-tional approaches, and Edward Long has succinctly summarized those characteristics thusly:

"1. A different starting point: Instead of the empirical examination of nature, turning to traditional authority to vindicate truths, or engagement in rational inquiry as a source of judgment, liberation theologies start with the experience of being marginalized or excluded.

2. A different interlocutor: Instead of the non-believer with intellectual difficulties about the viability of reli-gious faith, the interlocutor to whom liberation theolo-gies listen is the person (really a 'non-person') who has been crushed by or excluded from the surrounding social situation.

3. A different set of tools: Instead of philosophy, which uses the tools of metaphysical speculation and linguistic analysis, liberation theologians use the insights of sociologists and political thinkers (often of Marxists) to inquire concerning reality and to form concepts for describing and understanding it.

4. A different analysis: Instead of assuming that harmony is a normal condition between peoples and neutrality a clue to being fair and equitable, liberation theology regards conflict as a given corollary of injustice and looks upon identification with the oppressed in the struggle against injustice as the necessary way to overcome ideological blindness.

5. A different mode of engagement: Instead of search-ing for a theory the truth of which is settled as a first premise and then its implications drawn out, liberation theology works out truth and theory in continual

interrelationship with action and involvement. This is known as *praxis*.

6. A different theology: Instead of seeking understandings drawn from perceptions of 'the God above' (transcendent) and imposed on the world, theology becomes critical reflection on *praxis*, and develops from what we learn and experience by seeking to transform the world as Christians work (alongside of God) on behalf of the poor."[115]

Each of these characteristics can be illustrated by reference to the work of Cone and of Ruether. First, the starting point of liberation theology: Cone clearly states that, while theology does draw upon Scripture and tradition as sources of its insights, a third source is crucial for obtaining the proper vantage point upon Scipture and tradition, viz., the experience of the oppressed.[116] For Cone, this means that his theology will arise out of the concrete experiences of the black people. Furthermore, the modes of expression utilized by these people, their own unique stories and music, must not be overlooked. Similarly, Ruether avows that feminist theology must start with the experience of women.[117] And if this is the principle from which feminist theology proceeds, it follows, suggests Ruether, that in addition to traditional sources for Christian thought such as Scripture and the classical pronouncements of Catholicism, Orthodoxy, and Protestantism, the feminist theologian can rightfully appropriate the insights of "heretical" Christian traditions—she mentions Gnosticism, Montanism, Quakerism, and Shakerism—and of non-Christian Near Eastern and Greco-Roman religion and philosophy.[118]

As for the interlocutor: it is obvious that Cone and Ruether are concerned to address not the cultured despisers of religion but, rather, those persons who have been marginalized by oppressive social structures. Cone is especially concerned with black Americans, Ruether with women.

Cone and Ruether each make good use of tools different from those employed by more traditional theological thinkers: we see Cone building upon sociopolitical thought when he makes the all-important distinction between ideology and social a priori. Ideology, explains Cone, "is deformed thought, meaning that a certain idea or ideas are nothing but the function of the subjective interest of an individual or group. Truth therefore becomes what an individual wishes it to be as defined in accordance with a person's subjective

desires."[119] A social a priori, on the other hand, is "the
axiological grid without which thought cannot exist.
Social determination deals with the formation of
thought, the base from which thought's categories
emerge. This is what sociologists of knowledge mean
when they contend that social reality precedes thinking
[an axiological grid is the set of socially derived ideas
and values that one presupposes as fundamental and self-
evident and which structures all one's thinking about the
world]."[120] In short, if one's thinking is ideological, that
means that it has been distorted by one's socio-
economic-racial vantage point. But if one's thinking is
conditioned by a social a priori, which all thought must
be, this simply means that one always sees from a
particular vantage point, but this vantage point need not
distort one's thinking. For Cone, the vantage point of
white European and American theologians is ideological,
whereas the vantage point of the black oppressed is a
social a priori that, far from obstructing one's vision, is a
precondition for correctly comprehending the Christian
gospel. This is so because the biblical message centers
on the good news of God's liberation of the oppressed.

A perusal of Ruether's *Sexism and God-Talk* reveals
her use of tools such as sociology of knowledge,
contemporary ecological thought, and socio-economic
analysis. As for the particular tool mentioned above,
viz., Marxism, Ruether designates it one of the "modern
post-Christian resources for feminist theology"[121], and
Cone, in his later work, attempts a serious dialogue with
Marxism.[122]

We come next to the different analysis: here the best
example is probably Cone's position on the Christian
notion of violence. Consistent with Brown's formulation,
Cone holds that there is no such thing as a neutral
position outside the arena of conflict. The very fabric of
our unjust society is permeated with conflict and
violence. Hence, says Cone, "I contend that every one is
violent, and to ask, 'Are you nonviolent?' is to accept
the oppressors' values. Concretely, ours is a situation in
which the only option we have is that of deciding whose
violence we will support—that of the oppressors or the
oppressed."[123] The genuine distinction lies not between
violence and nonviolence, but between just violence and
unjust violence.

The fifth characteristic, undoubtedly one of the most
crucial, has to do with *praxis*: once again, examples are
easy to come by in both Cone and Ruether. For
instance, according to Cone, ". . . truth is not an

intellectual datum that is entrusted to academic guilds.
Truth cannot be separated from the people's struggle and
the hopes and dreams that arise from that struggle.
Truth is that transcendent reality, disclosed in the
people's historical struggle for liberation, which enables
them to know that their fight for freedom is not
futile."[124] As for Ruether, the integral character of
praxis is evident in her declaration that "the critical
principle of feminist theology is the promotion of the full
humanity of women. . . . whatever diminishes or denies
the full humanity of women must be presumed not to
reflect the divine or an authentic relation to the divine,
or to reflect the authentic nature of things. . . . This
negative principle also implies the positive principle:
what does promote the full humanity of women is of the
Holy."[125] The criteria for distinguishing the divine from
the demonic are worked out in the context of concrete
action. One might argue that this *praxis* orientation of
liberation theology provides a way around the Kantian
strictures against knowledge of God, not only in that it
seeks indirect rather than direct access to the infinite—
recall the relevant remarks about Soloveitchik above—
but also insofar as it suggests that Kant's epistemology is
invalid precisely because he failed to take account of the
rootedness of all knowing in a concrete context of action.

And this takes us to the final characteristic: instead of
a theology "from above," which imposes an alien
revelation upon actual mundane existence, liberation
theology is a theology "from below." Another way to
express the same thing is to say that liberation theology
is genuinely correlative, insofar as it derives what it has
to say about the divine from what it perceives to be the
divine impact upon human experience. This seems
clearly to be the case in Ruether's feminist theology.
Her notion of God/ess, the Primal Matrix, always has to
do with the experience of the marginalized, especially
women. It is perhaps less clearly the case in Cone's
theology. On the one hand, Cone certainly emphasizes
praxis and the need to see God from the perspective of
the oppressed, specifically, North American blacks. But,
on the other hand, much of what he has to say about
God seems to be presupposed as part of the content of
Christian faith. He tells us, for instance, that "the
identification of the story of liberation with God's story,
which troubles my critics, is not derived from the human
situation. Christian theology does not move from human
needs to God, but from God's revelation to our
needs."[126] It takes but a little imagination to see Karl

Barth, the subject of Cone's doctoral dissertation, wispering in Cone's ear at this point.

Of course, Cone can attempt to avoid the charge of fideism, that is, leaping into a closed circle of faith, by claiming that this problematic content of faith is presupposed precisely by that black community which is the concrete point of departure for his theology. But some commentators seem unconvinced. Cornel West, for one, himself a proponent of black theology, has expressed his reservations in no uncertain terms: ". . . Cone's religious claims reek of a hermetic fideism."[127] While one might expect white theologians, and perhaps even some black thinkers, to have a vested interest in the structures that Cone attacks and thus to look for ways to critique the socio-political implications of his thought, the relevant issue for our purposes is this spectre of fideism. It must be emphasized that this purported weakness in Cone's approach has to do not with the fact that he champions some of the tenets of classical Christian theology but, rather, with how he apparently imports those tenets into his his thought.

In our analysis of Joseph Soloveitchik's *Halakhic Man*, we noted the possiblity of taking Soloveitchik's description of halakhic existence as a phenomenological exhibition of the ability of the Halakhah to conquer the fundamental threats arising from our finitude and thus as evidence that the Halakhah manifests the infinite. Of course, this involved claims that, for the most part, had to do not with the nature of the infinite in and of itself, but with the Halakhah as the action of the divine in the finite world. Could we not make an analogous case for the liberation theology of Ruether and Cone, especially if we were to bracket those potentially problematic moments in Cone's theology where he claims to derive quite specific components of classical Christian thought from the experience of the oppressed? In other words, if the notions of the divine set forth by Ruether and Cone, when used by oppressed persons as the key to interpreting and forming their own experience, do prove to be transformative, not just vis-a-vis the Tillichian anxieties but also over against what Tillich might call the threat of nonbeing as it is manifest on the social-structural level—recall that the threat of nonbeing is a function of our being finite—wouldn't it be reasonable to conclude that those notions of the divine genuinely show the infinite?

Certainly Cone and Ruether attempt to obey the demand of the *logos* formula to expain *what* they claim to know and *how* they claim to know it. Do they also adhere to the principle of universal accountability? One can easily imagine a critic answering that the whole notion of theology arising from out of a particular situation, viz., the concrete experience of the oppressed, violates the demand for universal accountability. But it seems to me that liberation theologians like Ruether and Cone can prove this objection groundless. First of all, they can respond that there is, after all, no such thing as a theology that arises from nowhere, conditioned by no social a priori. As it turns out, liberation theology is perhaps simply more cognizant of, and thus less naive about, the actual starting point of theological reflection than are other theologies. As Ralph Ellison observed about the novel, one can arrive at the universal only through the particular. "All novels," says Ellison, "are about certain minorities: the individual is a minority. The universal in the novel. . . is reached only through the depiction of the specific man in a specific circumstance."[128] Furthermore, are not all persons, or at the very least all Americans, involved in the situations that Cone and Ruether describe? Of course white men, for instance, are not involved *in the same way* as are blacks and women. But precisely to the extent that white men are conceived as oppressors, they must also be conceived to have a crucial point of contact with the situation of the oppressed.

Perhaps one might object that liberation theologians cannot adhere to the principle of universal accountability insofar as different liberation theologies represent different situations of oppression. To take only our own two examples, Cone speaks for American blacks, and Ruether speaks for women. But this would be to construe Cone and Ruether too narrowly. In *My Soul Looks Back*, for example, Cone attempts a dialogue with such other varieties of liberation thought as Latin American liberation theology, feminist liberation theology, and Marxism.[129] And Ruether's interest in all marginalized persons, and even nonhuman nature, is readily apparent. Given current trends, it seems reasonable to expect an ever-increasing confluence of liberation perspectives.[130]

All in all, then, it appears that liberation theology, as represented by the thought of James Cone and Rosemary Radford Ruether, has as good a claim as the theologies of Whitehead, Rahner, and Soloveitchik to be considered a viable academic theology. But we must turn now to a theologian who takes the lessons of concrete historical and political experience every bit as seriously as do Cone and Ruether and, yet, comes to some very different conclusions.

6. Richard Rubenstein (1924-   )

In a passage so often quoted as to dull its impact, the German philosopher and essayist Friedrich Nietzsche announced that "God is dead."[131] For Nietzsche, as for the many others who have concurred with his assessment, belief in God is no longer tenable. But despite the prevelance of the conviction that we live in the time of the death of God, it is still surprising to find adherents of Christianity and Judaism, indeed "theologians" from those traditions, echoing Nietzsche's proclamation. During the 1960's, a number of theological positions appeared that were loosely collected under the rubric "radical theology" or the "death of God theology." The impetus to engage in this unusual brand of theologizing had various sources, from a consideration of the implications of contemporary philosophy to an infatuation with secularity and technology. I think many would agree with Langdon Gilkey's evaluation, according to which "the most compelling of the radical theologians. . . is Rabbi Richard L. Rubenstein, whose book *After Auschwitz* appeared late in 1966."[132] Rubenstein's conviction that the God of traditional Jewish piety is dead arises not out of some naive attachment to the promises of modern secular society nor from an examination of events that have since faded in their importance. Rather, his reflections are spurred by the terror of the Nazi Holocaust, Hitler's slaughter of six million Jews. As Rubenstein sees it, "Although Jewish history is replete with disaster, none has been so radical in its total import as the holocaust. Our images of God, man, and the moral order have been permanently impaired. No Jewish theology will possess even a remote degree of relevance to contemporary Jewish life if it ignores the question of God and the death camps. That is *the* question for Jewish theology in our times."[133] To the extent that it arises out of a confrontation with the concrete events of recent history, Rubenstein's thought has much in common with liberation theology.

The God that Rubenstein holds must now be rejected is the God traditionally embraced by Jews (and by Christians and Muslims as well), the God of history who providentially orders the events that constitute the human drama. For if one believes that such a God exists, one can only interpret the Holocaust as ordained by this God. But surely that conclusion is unacceptable, even morally repugnant. What could possibly justify a God sanctioning something like the Holocaust? No good that might arise out of the Holocaust, no punishment for sin, no lesson for humankind, would ever compensate for the suffering and death of its victims.

This does not mean, however, that Rubenstein is willing to go the way of contemporary secularism. He has no intention of cutting himself off from that Jewish religious heritage which defines his very being. As a consequence, Rubenstein still perceives a need to talk about God, the *what* of theological knowledge, even if it is not the God of history. He looks to "a mystical paganism which utilizes the historic forms of Jewish religion."[134] The heart of what Rubenstein dubs paganism is an intuition of "the primordial powers of earth and fatality."[135] Paganism replaces the God of history with the God of nature, the fecund ground from out of which life arises and to which it inevitably returns in death, the Earth as "cannibal Mother."[136] For Rubenstein, "Paganism is not a vulgar appeal to what is base in men; it is a wise intuition of man's place in the order of things."[137] In other words, the paganism Rubenstein favors allows us to acknowledge our finitude and our bondage to the earth.

Despite its pagan character, Rubenstein's God, like the God of history to which Jews have traditionally devoted themselves, is one rather than many: "The unity of God will continue to be maintained, for the Lord of history has given us insight into the partial and tentative character of all polytheistic representations of the life and source of the cosmos."[138] The awe-inspiring One who confronts us as God after the death of the God of history can properly be named the Holy Nothingness, the Holy Abyss. We approach this One as a *mysterium tremendum et fascinans*, Rudolf Otto's designation for the divine mystery that we find both attractive and repelling at one and the same time.[139] To return to the Holy Abyss out of which all finite things arise is to die, and death is something which, as Freud made clear, we both long for and fear; *eros*, the life-drive, always competes with the desire to return to the peaceful oblivion of death, *thanatos*. While it obviously grounds no ecstasy but, at best, only a happy nihilism, Rubenstein's Holy Nothingness is not without its parallels to the Holy Nothingness of the Jewish mystical tradition. There too life is lived in the tension between the desire to be an independent reality and the desire to be absorbed back into the Source from whence all things come.[140] It is in this sense that Rubenstein's "mystical paganism" is mystical.

For Rubenstein, then, it is only in death that the frustrations of finite existence will be transcended. Thus, "Death is the true Messiah and the land of the dead the place of God's true Kingdom."[141] It is mere illusion to hope for a literal New Jerusalem in which life will be lived without the terrors of finite existence. How does all of this square with the expectation that God, however God be conceived, should possess the power to deliver human beings from the Tillichian anxieties? It is obvious that Rubenstein's God cannot provide a life beyond the dilemmas of finitude. Rubenstein holds that nothing can provide such a life. Nonetheless, his God offers us a way of facing up to and dealing with our finitude. God is "the infinite measure against which we can see our own limited finite lives in proper perspective."[142] One is thus led to resign herself to the limitations of human existence, to "love his necessities."[143] More fully, Jews after Auschwitz "have lost all hope and faith. We have also lost all possibility of disappointment. Expecting absolutely nothing from God or man, we rejoice in whatever we receive. We have learned the nakedness of every human pretense. No people has come to know as we have how deeply man is an insubstantial nothingness before the awesome and terrible majesty of the Lord. We accept our nothingness—nay, we even rejoice in it— for in finding our nothingness we have found both ourselves and the God who alone is true substance. We did not ask to be born; we did not ask for our absurd existence in the world; nor have we asked for the fated destiny which has hung about us as Jews. Yet we would not exchange it, nor would we deny it, for when nothing is asked for, nothing is hoped for, nothing is expected; all that we receive is truly grace."[144] There is clearly a sense, then, in which Rubenstein's Holy Nothingness displays its infinity over against the finitude manifest in ontic, moral, and spiritual anxiety, insofar as existence before the Holy Nothingness puts our lives in perspective so that we creatively resign ourselves to our finitude and thereby achieve a sober kind of joy in living.

Rubenstein does not expect, however, that the individual man or woman should stand before the Holy Nothingness and face his or her finitude alone. Thus, despite his rejection of the traditional Jewish God, Rubenstein by no means rejects the synagogue and the traditional rituals enacted there. As a matter of fact, he prizes myth and ritual more highly than the moral exhortation that is heard in the synagogue and that is often taken to be the essence of Judaism. He explains, "We need the religious institution. . . precisely because the human condition is unredeemed in the present and ultimately hopeless in what lies beyond the existential horizon. . . . Religion cannot be indifferent to social justice but neither can its major task be equated with its pursuit. The primary role of religion is priestly. It offers men a ritual and mythic structure in which the abiding realities of life and death can be shared. As long as men are born, pass through the crises of transition in life, experience guilt, fail—as fail they must—grow old, and die, traditional churches and synagogues will be irreplaceable institutions."[145] Rubenstein is especially sensitive to the jumble of forces and fears that constitute the human psyche—recall the discussion of *eros* and *thanatos* above—and he holds that traditional religious myths and rites are powerful tools for dealing with those forces and fears, both conscious and unconscious. His reading of the psyche makes it apparent that, while liberation theologians frequently draw on the philosophy of Marx to guide their thinking, Rubenstein's analysis of the human condition takes its bearings from the work of Freud.

The *what* of Rubenstein's theology is now clearly in view: the true God is the Abyss out of which all beings come and to which they must return in death. This Holy Nothingness confronts the individual human being with his or her finitude and, with the aid of the myths and rituals of the religious community, enables the individual to accept that finitude. What, then, can be said of the *how* of Rubenstein's theology? His contention that the Nothingness that surrounds human existence should be paid the homage due divinity is based not only on the fact that Nothingness is both our ultimate source and our ultimate destination, but also on the claim that this Nothingness can effect a creative human response to the anxieties associated with finitude. Thus, there is a similarity with the correlative *how* that we suggested is present in both Soloveitchik and liberation theology: one attempts to grasp the being of the infinite by noting its concrete effects upon human finitude, specifically, upon the anxieties and threats that spring from finitude. While the deities of Whitehead and Rahner are said to have the ability to conquer these same anxieties and threats, the existence of those deities is argued on other grounds. If God exists, says Rahner, he can effectively address the dilemmas resulting from our finitude, and the fact that he does exist is established by a transcendental analysis of human knowledge and action. If God exists, suggests Whitehead, he can help human beings counter the threats arising from finitude, and the fact that he does exist is made apparent via the method of descriptive generalization. By contrast, we have read Soloveitchik, liberation theology, and now Rubenstein as suggesting that the anxieties associated with finitude are, in certain specific circumstances, actually allayed and that this fact points to the reality of the infinite that negates the inherent weaknesses of finitude.

But what is perhaps more interesting is an earlier moment in the *how* of theological knowledge as employed by Rubenstein: before we turn to Nothingness and pronounce it Holy, we must reject the Lord of history, the traditional God of Judaism and of the religions that grow out of Judaism. How do we come to recognize the necessity of abandoning the God of history? We do so, says Rubenstein, by taking with utmost seriousness what is called the problem of theodicy, the problem of justifying belief in a compassionate and omnipotent Providence in the face of suffering and evil. Specifically, we recognize that no such Providence could possibly have guided the history that led to Auschwitz. The thesis that there exists a benevolent and all-powerful deity is falsified by the facts of human experience.

This component of Rubenstein's *how* is fascinating if for no other reason than that it suggests that, contrary to the claims of some philosophers, theistic beliefs are not necessarily so vacuous that they are consistent with all possible experiences and, hence, unfalsifiable.[146] One of the most effective and familiar statements of this alleged difficulty with theism is Antony Flew's version of the parable of the invisible gardener: "Once upon a time two explorers came upon a clearing in the jungle. In the clearing were growing many flowers and many weeds. One explorer says, 'Some gardener must tend this plot.' The other disagrees, 'There is no gardener.' So they pitch their tents and set a watch. No gardener is ever seen. 'But perhaps he is an invisible gardener.' So they set up a barbed-wire fence. They electrify it. They patrol with bloodhounds. (For they remember how H.G. Wells's *The Invisible Man* could be both smelt and touched though he could not be seen.) But no shrieks ever suggest that some intruder has received a shock. No movements of the wire ever betray an invisible climber. The bloodhounds never give cry. Yet still the Believer is not convinced. 'But there is a gardener, invisible, intangible, insensible to electric shocks, a gardener who has no scent and makes no sound, a gardener who comes secretly to look after the garden which he loves.' At last the Sceptic despairs, 'But what remains of your original assertion? Just how does what you call an invisible, intangible, eternally elusive gardener differ from an imaginary gardener or even from no gardener at all?' "[147] In other words, if one who believes in the existence of God so construes God that his existence is consistent with any possible experience, i.e., so that no experience could falsify the claim that such a God exists, then the believer seems really to be asserting nothing at all. Rubenstein does not fall into this dilemma. Rather, he abandons belief in the traditional God of Western religion because he thinks that there are in fact human experiences that give the lie to that belief. The existence of the God of history is simply not consistent with the suffering and evil of Auschwitz; the characteristics of the God of history are sufficiently specific for certain historical events to count against his existence. Of course, many other thinkers would argue that there are theologically more profitable responses to the kind of dilemma that Flew poses than the response of ceasing to believe in the God of history. For instance, many have criticized Flew's notion of what constitutes meaningful assertions as naive and inadequate. But Rubenstein must at least be given credit for having refused to sidestep this challenge to theology.

What about universal accountability? We have noted that one part of Rubenstein's *how* is parallel to that of Soloveitchik and liberation theology: we have read him as suggesting that one can see the potency of his version of the infinite by observing its concrete effect upon finite existence. If Rubenstein is in fact able to display that effect, we must grant that he observes the demand for universal accountability. Another component of the *how* is, as we have seen, a juxtaposition of the human suffering evinced by recent history with the belief in an omnipotent, loving Providence. Surely there is no transgression of the principle of universal accountability here, for the facts of history are open to all.

Of course, the interpretation of the facts of history may vary. Clearly, the Jewish community has a different relation to them than other groups. Has Rubenstein read the significance of Auschwitz for Judaism correctly? He obviously regards it as decisive, a watershed event that forces the Jew to radically rethink his or her notion of the divine. Not all Jewish commentators agree with Rubenstein's assessment. Jacob Neusner, for example, asks, "What then are the implications of the Holocaust? I claim there is *no* implication—none for Judaic theology, none for Jewish community life—which was not present before 1933. . . . In fact Judaic piety has all along known how to respond to disaster. For those for whom the classic Judaic symbolic structure remains intact, the wisdom of the classic piety remains sound. For those to whom classical Judaism offers no viable option, the Holocaust changes nothing. One who did not believe in God before he knew about the Holocaust is not going to be persuaded to believe in Him on its account. One who believed in the classical perception of God presented by Judaic theologians is not going to be forced to change his perception on its account."[148] According to Neusner, Rubenstein's reading of the Holocaust, which Neusner clearly regards as an over-reading, has more to do with the tensions and doubts that plagued American society in the Vietnam era than with the characteristics of the Holocaust itself. Jewish piety has been faced with overwhelming evil many times in its history; the Holocaust is not qualitatively different.

What would Rubenstein say to such a charge? Would he not have to admit that Job, the righteous man whom the Hebrew Bible tells us suffered horribly and inexplicably, posed the very same question to God that arises from the Holocaust: Why have you decreed that I should suffer thus? And isn't it true that, in spite of his suffering, Job did not abandon belief in the God of history? Rubenstein holds that it is "a very serious mistake to believe that Job can serve as a model for the Jewish religious response to Auschwitz. . . . There can be a question for Job only when there is a Job. Hideously afflicted, Job sat on his dung heap. No matter how terrible his condition became, he was at all times recognized as a person by both God and man. At Auschwitz, the Jew did no sit upon the dung heap. He became less than the dung heap. At least the dung heap has the ability to expand earth's life-giving capacity. No

'Thou' was addressed to the Auschwitz Jew by either God or man. The Jew became a nonperson in the deepest sense. Neither his life nor his death mattered. There was no question because there was no Job. Job went up in smoke. His question went with him."[149] No matter how horrible the enemies that the Jewish community faced in the past, says Rubenstein, those enemies sought only the defeat of the Jews, not their removal from the face of the earth, not genocide.

If there is disagreement between Rubenstein and other Jewish thinkers as to how Jews should evaluate the Holocaust theologically, there are apparently also discrepancies between what Rubenstein gleans from the history of humankind, ancient and modern, and what liberation theologians glean. For instance, while one might be able to find at least some similarities between Rosemary Radford Ruether's Primal Matrix and Richard Rubenstein's Holy Nothingness, it is clear that Rubenstein's Nothingness is a far cry from James Cone's God of the oppressed. Cone's God is the very God of history that Rubenstein says recent history makes untenable. Both Cone and Rubenstein provide an account of *what* they believe they know and *how* they believe they know it that is, at least for the most part, universally available. And their respective accounts of the *how* both draw upon the lessons of concrete historical existence. Why, then, are their accounts of the *what* so different? Someone may respond that, while Christians find God present as liberator in their experience, the same God has abandoned the Jews, but such a response will be accepted only by the morally comatose. That two theologians can be equally observant of what we are calling the *logos* formula and nonetheless arrive at contradictory conclusions is a dilemma that we shall have to take up in Chapter Four. In the meantime, we must move from Rubenstein's Holy Nothingness to Nāgārjuna's emptiness.

7. Nāgārjuna (circa A.D. 150-250)

We have already encountered a diversity of perspectives on the *what* of theological knowledge. There is obviously a significant difference, for example, between the infinite manifest in the relatively traditional Western conception of God set forth by Cone and the infinite revealed in Rubenstein's radical notion of the Holy Nothingness. But Nāgārjuna will lead us even further away from familiar Western conceptions of *theos*. For Nāgārjuna, a seminal Buddhist thinker, while the goal of the religious quest might well be deemed infinite, it cannot be called "God." *Theos* as he conceives it is much more accurately translated with the word "emptiness."

In the analysis that follows, I shall rely heavily upon Frederick Streng's interpretation of Nāgārjuna.[150] Streng's approach is useful for our purposes, first of all, in that he limits his investigation "to conceptual expressions which are formulations that can be denied, attacked, defended, and explained."[151] In other words, he concentrates on formulations that express a way of thinking; he suggests that Nāgārjuna's position is a candidate for the sort of theology that we are pursuing. Second, Streng shows that Nāgārjuna's position aims at an ultimate transformation of the individual human being. This will aid in our grasp of the *how* of Nāgārjuna's theological knowledge, and it will serve as a point of contact between Nāgārjuna's position and those of Soloveitchik, the liberation theologians, and Rubenstein.

As a Buddhist, Nāgārjuna begins, in essence, with the Four Noble Truths believed to have been articulated by Gautama: first, existence is characterized by suffering or turmoil. Second, this turmoil results from the individual's attachment to objects that are, in reality, fabrications of human intellect and emotion. Third, it is possible to escape turmoil. Fourth, freedom or escape is achieved by following the path marked out by the Buddha.

According to the Buddhist, the world we see around us in our everyday mode of apprehension is a merely conventional world, in that the objects which make it up are the product of the conventions of human thinking and willing. We shape the contours of the world through our categorizations and evaluations. Even the notion of the self as a constant, substantial reality is a fabrication. What is more, the objects that we fabricate cause turmoil because they produce in us attitudes such as desire and revulsion. We are attached to the realm of objects. Thus, existence is colored by greed, struggle, and misery. The misery in particular is powerfully represented in the story of the Four Passing Sights mentioned in Chapter One: the Buddha saw an old man, a diseased man, a dead man, and a monk. The first three of these sights correspond to Tillich's ontic anxiety, insofar as old age and disease are objects of the relative form of ontic anxiety and death is the object of the absolute form.

If one succeeds in traversing the Buddhist path, he or she will attain *nirvana*, the extinction of the ego and its fabrications, the dissolution of the bonds of finitude. Because *nirvana* stands outside the discriminations and oppositions that characterize our fabrication of the conventional world, it is not susceptible to description. *Nirvana*, then, might be judged a kind of nothingness. Streng makes it clear, however, that the nothingness at which Nāgārjuna aims is neither the nothingness of nihilism nor the nothingness of pure being. One might well regard Rubenstein's theology as a species of nihilism. It is a perspective according to which the world of our existence is suspended above an abyss. Everything that is finds both its source and its ultimate destination in a realm of nonbeing. At the opposite end of the continuum from this nihilism one finds a philosophy that looks to a realm of pure being which transcends the world of our existence. Because it is an absolute fullness, one can make no statements that characterize pure being. It does not possess certain specific characteristics and lack others. Thus, it is a nothingness for human thought. This nothingness is the goal of most mystics, those religious questers who wish to be absorbed into an incomprehensible godhead.

But Nāgārjuna has no interest in a separate realm outside the world of our existence, whether that realm is conceived as the abyss of nonbeing or the fullness of pure being. For him, the crucial distinction is not between two realities, but two kinds of truth: conventional truth, which characterizes our everyday apprehension of reality, and Ultimate Truth, which gets at the same reality in a wholly different fashion. The key to his thinking is the term "*śūnyatā*," that is, "emptiness." The Ultimate Truth is that all things are empty, they have no independent reality, no self-existence. Therefore, the *what* of Nāgārjuna's theological knowledge is not some Ultimate Reality. Instead, it is Ultimate Truth, a way of perceiving reality such that one recognizes the objects that make up reality to be mere fabrications, the attachment to which produces turmoil. For Nāgārjuna, even *nirvana* is empty. If we were to reify *nirvana* as some kind of ultimate *thing* to be attained, we would become attached to it in the same way that we become attached to other things. We would be anxious about possessing it. Thus, *nirvana* would function, paradoxically enough, as a source of turmoil.

Streng explains clearly the place of Ultimate Truth and of conventional or mundane truth in Nāgārjuna's philosophy: "Mundane truth is based on the intellectual and emotional attachment to ideas or sense objects whereby such objects of knowledge were used as if they had an existence independent of the perceiver. Such truth discriminates, identifies, and categorizes segments of existence as 'door,' 'room,' 'money,' 'I,' 'you,' or any mental or sensual object of cognition. All men use such truth to carry on the everyday affairs of life. Likewise *all* religious doctrines and theories about the nature of existence fall within the bounds of mundane truth, for they are fabrications. Ultimate Truth, on the other hand, is a quality of life expressed in the complete indifference to the construction or cessation of 'things'. . . . Nāgārjuna accepted the practical distinction between the two kinds of truth, and because this was only a practical distinction he felt free to use mundane truth, that required logical and semantic conventions, to dispel the attachment to the products of this truth and thereby lead the religious student toward Ultimate Truth."[152] Nāgārjuna recognizes his own conceptual formulations as empty, as mere fabrications, but he believes that he can use these fabrications to spur his listener to recognize the emptiness of all things and thus to free himself or herself from turmoil.

Suppose we consider the conceptual formulations Nāgārjuna uses to effect a recognition of *śūnyatā*. Nāgārjuna employs what Streng terms a "negative dialectic." The word "dialectic" here refers to the movement of Nāgārjuna's argument. It is negative in that it "denies the ultimate validity of any view"[153] and reveals "the self-negating character of logical inference."[154] Note, for example, what happens when Nāgārjuna turns his dialectic upon the "thing" we call space: "Space does not exist at all before the defining characteristic of space. If it would exist before the defining characteristic, then one must falsely conclude that there would be something without a defining characteristic. In no case has anything existed without a defining characteristic. If an entity without a defining characteristic does not exist, to what does the defining characteristic apply? Therefore space is neither an existing thing nor a non-existing thing, neither something to which a defining characteristic applies nor a defining characteristic."[155] This quotation illustrates the fact that Nāgārjuna seeks a so-called "middle way." Edward Conze explains it thus: "*Emptiness* here means the identity of yes and no. In this system of thought the gentle art of undoing with one hand what one has done with the other is considered as the very quintessence of fruitful living. . . . *Emptiness* is that which stands right in the middle between affirmation and negation, existence and non-existence, eternity and annihilation. The germ of this idea is found in an early saying, which the scriptures of all [Buddhist] schools have transmitted. The Buddha says to Katyayana that the world usually bases its views on two things, existence and non-existence. 'It is,' is one extreme; 'it is not' is another. Between those two limits the world is imprisoned. The holy men transcend this limitation."[156] Nāgārjuna's use of negative dialectic points out this middle way and thereby indicates that the fabrications of conventional thinking are empty.

The fact that the "things" round about us have no independent reality is reenforced by the doctrine of dependent co-origination. It holds that each "thing" that we find in the world is what it is only in relation to other "things." Here again, Conze's explanation is clear and to the point: "Any relative thing is functionally dependent on other things, and can exist, and be conceived, only in and through its relations with other things. By itself it is nothing, it has no separate inward reality."[157] And insofar as "things" have no separate inward reality, they are empty. Once again, we see how inferences based on the logical rules of conventional thinking can undo that thinking and reveal that the objects of conventional thinking have no self-existence.

If the negative dialectic and the doctrine of dependent co-origination are merely tools which themselves are empty, what is supposed to follow upon their use? Some interpreters have suggested that Nāgārjuna uses these tools in order to clear away all thought and leave room for an intuition, i.e., a suprarational apprehension, of a reality that transcends the finite, empty world.[158] But as we noted above, following Frederick Streng, Nāgārjuna holds not that there are two kinds of reality, but that there are two kinds of truth. Hence, there is no Absolute beyond the everyday world. Nāgārjuna takes the middle way even when discussing emptiness itself: "One may not say that there is 'emptiness,' nor that there is 'non-emptiness.' Nor that both exist simultaneously, nor that neither exists; the purpose for saying 'emptiness' is only for the purpose of conveying knowledge."[159] Tools such as the negative dialectic and the doctrine of dependent co-origination and words such as "emptiness" convey knowledge. However, they do so not by pointing to an object with which they correspond, but by indicating that we should take on a new attitude toward the world. Streng holds that what is involved here is nothing less than a kind of knowledge that is coextensive with one's mode of existence. In other words, what one knows is what one becomes. He suggests, "The English word 'realize' captures the two elements in the sense that man can be said to 'realize' certain possibilities. He both 'knows' and 'becomes' the possibilities."[160] Nāgārjuna's arguments are intended to make us realize—i.e., know—that everything we encounter is empty, so that we can realize—i.e., effect or live out—freedom from desire and attachment.

Because our attachment to the fabrications that constitute the conventional world is the root of all our turmoil, freedom from that attachment is tantamount to what Streng terms "ultimate transformation."[161] Quite simply, "The apprehension of emptiness is a solution to all problems, not because 'a solution' has been found, but because the problems have ceased to be 'problems.' "[162] The suffering that accompanies finitude, e.g. the suffering the Buddha encountered in the first three Passing Sights, is transcended.

The *what* of Nāgārjuna's theological knowledge is the Ultimate Truth that all things are empty and the freedom that follows from a realization of Ultimate Truth. It seems fair to say that this *what* is infinite. For while we have followed Streng in suggesting that Nāgārjuna does not point to an infinite *being* or *thing*, it is nonetheless clear that Nāgārjuna wishes to break the bonds of finitude and feels that the realization of emptiness accomplishes just that. Thus, the realization of emptiness must be said to effect a negation of the negativities of finite existence; while the realization of emptiness is not a matter of confronting an infinite substance, it does enable one to participate in a process that might legitimately be called the process of *infinition*, of overcoming the finite.

The *how* of Nāgārjuna's theological knowledge is, first of all, the negative dialectic that seeks to convince us that all things are empty. Secondly, Nāgārjuna can point to the ultimate transformation effected via the concrete recognition of emptiness. In this respect, the *how* that we find in Nāgārjuna is not unlike that present in Soloveitchik, the liberation theologians, and Rubenstein: the reality of the infinite, so one might argue, is concretely displayed in the conquest of those anxieties and threats that are rooted in the very nature of finitude.

If Nāgārjuna explains the *what* and the *how* of his theology, does he do so in a way that is consistent with the demand for universal accountability? It would seem so. After all, the grasp of his negative dialectic does not presuppose any special commitments. And while the ultimate transformation that is so central to his case can be concretely experienced only by those who walk the Buddhist path and fully realize emptiness, it is reasonable to assume that the outward effects of such a transformation—for instance, a supreme serenity in the face of the challenges of finitude—could be made apparent even to those who have not experienced it for themselves, by calling their attention to the life of a Buddhist who understands the emptiness of all things.

8.   Emmanuel Levinas (1906-   )

The demand for universal accountability arises both from within theology itself and from the larger social context provided by modernity and postmodernity, and all of the thinkers we have considered thus far accede to that demand, with the notable exception of Karl Barth. At the same time, perhaps no thinker has taken more seriously than Barth that other factor that we have noted springing from within theology and from without it: skepticism about our ability to attain knowledge of the infinite. There is a kind of symmetry in our beginning with Karl Barth and ending with Emmanuel Levinas, for Levinas too makes every effort to underline the absolute transcendence of the infinite beyond the finite. As Steven Smith has observed, Barth and Levinas share a concern with the *totaliter aliter*, the "wholly other."[163]

Levinas's thought is difficult, and his vocabulary is forbidding. Thus, we shall try to simplify our investigation of Levinas by selecting a single point of entry into his philosophy. That point of entry is a problem that is particularly evident in the modern and postmodern worlds, a problem that can be designated the tyranny of the human subject. Insofar as all experience of the world is experience had by a human person, the "subject" of the experience, it seems that, at least in a *practical* sense, reality is ultimately reducible to the human subject. I am the subject of all the objects that I experience; the objects of experience are "subjected" to my authority. When modern philosophers wish to analyze knowledge, they turn to a consideration of the human subject, a fact illustrated in our investigations of Kant and Rahner (recall what is involved in their transcendental methods) and Whitehead (remember his reformed subjectivist priniciple). Knowledge turns out to be a matter of the subject possessing the world. I can, as it were, possess everything that I can know, even "up to the remotest stars," as Levinas puts it.[164]

The problem here is that there seems to be no way to escape the vantage point of the subject, to get outside it and make immediate contact with the extra-subjective world. We find ourselves caught in a nihilistic perspective according to which the "alterity" or otherness of the world is drained away by the subject who experiences it. Otherness is reduced to the sameness of subjectivity. That this is so can be made evident by noting how understanding the world involves unifying it around the subject. A chaos of data does not equal understanding. Understanding arises only when the disparate data can be put together, and this requires that each bit of data is referred back to the same experiencing subject. In Kant's language, all understanding presupposes a "transcendental unity of apperception."[165]

The tyrannical character of the subject can also be illustrated via an analysis of how knowledge depends on the knowing subject's ability to reduce everything to the same time, the time of the subject: to know something is to hold it in mind, to encapsulate it in the "now" or "present" of my act of consciousness. Knowledge synchronizes the world, that is, brings all events, past and future, into the unity of the present moment of thinking. That is why it is appropriate for philosophers to say that thinking entails "representation." If, for example, I wish to think about Abraham Lincoln's presidency, I must represent it to myself in images and concepts, i.e., *re-present* it, make it present again. Thinking is thematization, the unification of diverse elements from diverse times and places into a single theme upon which the mind can dwell. Levinas sums up this dilemma for us: knowledge, he says, "is by essence a relation with what one equals and includes, with that

whose alterity one suspends, with what becomes immanent, because it is to my measure and to my scale. . . .
Knowledge is always an adequation between thought and
what it thinks. There is in knowledge, in the final
account, an impossibility of escaping the self."[166]

How can we escape the tyranny of the subject? Where
shall we find genuine transcendence? One might suppose
that escape and transcendence are to be found, if
anywhere, in what philosophers and theologians alike
ordinarily regard as the ultimate stratum of reality upon
which all else depends, viz., Being. While it may be true
that the *beings* that populate the world are subject to the
tyranny of our knowing grasp, surely both these beings
and we ourselves are, in turn, subject to *Being*, the
power of being that allows all beings to be. Must we not
conclude, therefore, that Being offers the transcendence
and the escape from tyranny that we seek? No, says
Levinas, for precisely as the One that unifies all beings,
Being quashes genuine alterity or otherness just like
thinking does. In fact, Being and thinking are simply
two sides of the same coin: Being is the source of the
totality of what is and, as such, a totalitarian synchronization that ever reduces the other to the same, that
harmonizes the many into a single theme.

Thus, following in the footsteps of his fellow Jewish
thinker Franz Rosenzweig, Levinas looks for a way
beyond even the totality that is Being.[167] As he
expresses it in the title of one of his books, he seeks
something "otherwise than Being."[168] Levinas finds what
he is looking for, a genuine infinity that wholly
transcends Being, in the realm of the ethical. The other
human being is truly Other, Other even than Being, for
this Other confronts me with *an infinite moral responsibility*. Put simply, "one is never quits with regard to the
Other."[169] Or, to employ the language of the Hebrew
Bible, I am my brother's keeper, and no amount of
action that I undertake on his behalf can ever discharge
my moral responsibility toward him. Thus, says Levinas,
my relation to the Other can be characterized with
images like that of the hostage: I am morally responsible
to give myself as hostage for the Other, to substitute
myself for him. This kind of radical imagery is intended
to express the fact that the infinity of my responsibility
to the Other explodes the confines of the unity of
thinking. Consciousness cannot contain an infinity; I
cannot put neatly into a theme something that has no
boundaries. The infinity of responsibility can be
expressed vis-a-vis the drive of thinking to synchronize

the world by saying that the Other confronts me as a reality that is always prior to my thinking. I am always already too late in my attempts to place my relation to the Other into the "now" of my consciousness. Levinas often puts it this way: the Other confronts me as a reality that is *diachronic*, i.e., never subject to the synchrony of my thought. Such baroque vocabulary is characteristic of Levinas, but we can perhaps understand his penchant for it by recognizing that he wants to express something that is wholly transcendent. For to the extent that the Other is beyond the tyranny of thinking's drive toward synchronization and thematization, the Other is also beyond even Being.

This absolute priority of the Other to my subjectivity is underscored in Levinas' claim that my responsibility to the Other, what might be called my openness to him or her, founds all other types of openness. For instance, it is only because I am made open to the Other man or woman that I can be aware of the material things around me: sense experience, which requires that I have the capacity to open myself to what exists in the material world outside myself, is founded upon my openness to the Other human being. In fact, Levinas holds that even the phenomenon of individuation, that is, my recognition that I am one particular being, unique and distinguishable from all other beings, is rooted in my moral responsibility to the Other. How so? The answer has to do with my inability to shift my moral responsibility onto someone else's shoulders. From the perspective afforded by this responsibility, I and I alone am responsible for my neighbor. Nothing that anyone else does can lessen what I am dutybound to do. And to the extent that the Other confronts me with this "I and I alone," he or she individuates me, calls me out of the undifferentiated background of the world into the foreground of uniqueness and individuality.

Suppose we respond to Levinas by saying that, while all of this is quite fascinating, it is merely unsubstantiated assertion. "Prove to us," so we might demand, "that every one of us has this infinite responsibility to every Other." How will Levinas reply? He might well respond, first, in a way that must strike us as frustratingly resistant to our grasp but nonetheless consistent with his position: the demand for some kind of proof of my infinite moral responsibility to the Other presupposes that such responsibility can be held within the confines of my consciousness so as to be measured against the criteria provided by my thinking. But this is just what can never be presupposed where responsibility to the Other is concerned. For, as we have seen, that responsibility exceeds any thematization, it has always already escaped my attempts at synchronization. The demand for proof is, in short, simply too late.

But, lacking the kind of evidence that one can try before the tribunal of thought so as to arrive at an incontrovertible verdict, Levinas can at least point us toward the concrete facts of our encounter with the Other. Observe, for instance, that when I come face to face with the Other, I feel a discomfort at my silence and am provoked to say something, even if I say nothing of any real consequence. "It is difficult to be silent in someone's presence. . . . It is necessary to speak of something, of the rain and fine weather, no matter what, but to speak, to respond to him and already to answer for him."[170] Note what Levinas is getting at here: it is quite right that the content of what I say is not significant. What is significant is just that I am driven to speak, i.e., I am driven to offer myself to the Other, to be open to his or her need, to acknowledge my responsibility for him or her.

Levinas insightfully expresses the import of this speaking to the Other by translating it with the sentence, "Here I am." For "Here I am" does not express a content, but rather my subjection to the other. This subjection is especially clear in Levinas' own French, where the sentence is rendered, "*me voici*." Here the pronoun "I" is in the accusative case rather than in the nominative, which means that the "I" is not really the subject of the action, but the object.[171] When I respond to the need to say something to the Other, i.e., when I say "Here I am," I am in essence responding to the infinite moral command that the Other represents for me, I am putting myself—or better, I am being put—at the Other's disposal. Thus, "Here I am" does not signify a content. That is, it does not signify in the sense of referring thought to some entity. Rather, it signifies in a much more primordial fashion: it refers me to the Other in the sense of making me the one responsible for the Other.

What are we to make, finally, of the infinity that confronts us in the face of the Other? Levinas answers that it is quite appropriate for us to use the word "God" at this point. He immediately cautions us, however, not to mistake how God fits in here. For it follows from what Levinas has told us about the infinity we encounter in the face of the Other that this infinity transcends both

beings and Being. And this means that it cannot
possibly be gathered into a theme and made an object of
consciousness. In fact, God is even further removed
from our grasp than is the Other! God directs us away
from himself to the Other. We respond to the divine
command which binds us to an infinite responsibility by
serving the Other. Levinas' language is characteristically
extreme: ". . . God is torn up from objectivity, presence
and Being. He is neither an object nor an interlocutor.
His absolute remoteness, his transcendence turns into my
responsibility. . . for the Other. And this analysis
implies that God is not simply the 'first Other' or the
'Other par excellence' or the 'absolutely Other,' but
other than the Other, other otherwise, other with an
alterity prior to the alterity of the Other, prior to the
ethical bond with another, and different from every
neighbor, transcendent to the point of absence. . . ."[172]
Levinas is trying to make it clear that we do not get to
the reality of God by reasoning that there must be some
absolute, divine Other behind the human Other. Our
relation to God is much less direct than even that kind
of indirect relation. Part of Levinas' concern here is
undoubtedly to distinguish his own talk of God from
that of another influential Jewish thinker, Martin Buber,
who speaks of the Eternal Thou who stands behind
every human Thou.[173]

If God is so totally resistant to our grasp, how can we
talk about him at all? We cannot talk about him in a
representational language which functions to present to
our thinking an object named by that language. God-
talk can only be testimony, that is, an indirect reference
to God constituted simply by an acknowledgment of
having been commanded to take on an infinite responsibility. It is the "Here I am," proffered to the neighbor,
that renders such testimony. Recall that, in essence,
"Here I am" communicates no content, but is equivalent
to my being put at the neighbor's disposal. Thus,
Levinas can say that "when in the presence of the Other,
I say 'Here I am!', this 'Here I am!' is the place through
which the Infinite enters into language, but without
giving itself to be seen. Since it is not thematized. . . it
does not appear. The 'invisible God' is not to be
understood as God invisible to the senses, but as God
non-thematizable in thought. . . ."[174] In a move
reminiscent of rabbinic biblical interpretation, Levinas
refers us to the anthropomorphic story in the Hebrew
Bible according to which a disobedient Adam tried to
hide himself from God in the thickets of the Garden of

Eden but, when called by God, had, in essence, to acknowledge his ethical responsibility with the "Here I am." For Levinas, Adam can here be said to offer testimony to the reality of God.[175]

We are now at the point where we must attempt to sum up the *what* and the *how* of Levinas' theological thinking. While we have no direct access to the *what*, it is possible to say that it is the infinity of moral responsiblity that I encounter in the face of the Other person. When I submit to that responsibility, I testify to the reality of the divine. Because God is infinite, one is tempted to simply assume that Levinas would be happy to say that God conquers ontic, moral, and spiritual anxiety. But that assumption would be rash. It is not that Levinas' God is insufficiently transcendent and hence unable to address the anxieties that manifest human finitude. Rather, this God is so thoroughly transcendent, so wholly other, that we mistake our relation to him if we read him as a reality that will satisfy our drive towards the infinite, that will console us in our state of anxiety. We are not, after all, in a position to objectify God as the endpoint of our needs. We are subject to him, and he points us away from himself to our neighbor. As for ontic anxiety, for instance, Levinas points out that our infinite responsibility for the Other demands "a devotedness as strong as death, and in a sense stronger than death. . . . The tomb is not a refuge; it is not a pardon. The debt remains."[176] In Steven Smith's formulation, Levinas' position requires not only that we are ready to suffer, but that, in our readiness, we are "indifferent to the death of the self."[177] Nonetheless, the fact that Levinas' God transcends even the kind of infinite that addresses human anxiety by no means suggests that this God fails our test of infinity. The opposite is obviously the case: Levinas directs us to a God that appears to be even more radically infinite.

The *how* of Levinas' theology is more difficult to assess. We have already explored why he would reject calls to provide evidence of the infinity to which he points. Such calls are too late. The infinite demand has always already been placed upon me, and all of my attempts to bring it into the synchronicity of consciousness must therefore fail. Here again, the Bible comes to Levinas' aid, for he can refer us to the story in Exodus 33 about Moses' request to see God, to have God present himself.[178] There we learn that no human being can look upon God directly, but only upon the back of God, i.e., only upon God as already having passed by.

This suggests that God cannot be *directly* correlated with the human. Of the divine command Levinas says, "It is an august command, but one that does not constrain or dominate and leaves me outside of any correlation with its source."[179]

Nonetheless, Levinas is quite willing to point us to the place where we can indirectly encounter the infinity of the divine, viz., the face of the human Other. Thus, there is clearly an indirect correlation of the infinite and the finite in Levinas. And, in contrast to the theology of Karl Barth, the place that Levinas specifies as the locus of our indirect encounter with the divine is accessible to all persons in all times and places, just insofar as they come face to face with Others. Therefore, there can be no doubt that Levinas respects the demand for universal accountability. Indeed, it would be easy to interpret Levinas' theology as demanding such accountability.

Because one of our central concerns in this chapter has been to indicate the diversity of perspectives on the *what* and the *how* of theological knowledge, even among theologians who abide by the requirements of the *logos* formula, it is appropriate to conclude our look at Levinas by briefly comparing him to Rubenstein, for Levinas and Rubenstein might be said to arrive at different theologies while drawing upon the same tradition and experiences. Like Rubenstein, Levinas is a Jew. And although, unlike Rubenstein, he is not a rabbi, Levinas is steeped in the traditions of the Jewish faith. He has written extensively on the rabbinic commentary known as the Talmud. Clearly, Levinas sees his philosphy as consistent with the spirit of the Talmud, for, in Steven Smith's words, "the Talmud names God by exploring relations with beyond-Being. . . and the holiness of God is found to refer directly to the constitution of a just society."[180] What is more, the Nazi Holocaust has played a powerful part in the formation of Levinas' thinking. Levinas, who emigrated from Lithuania to France, lost all of the members of his Lithuanian family in the Holocaust, and he has con- fessed that his intellectual biography "is dominated by the presentiment and the memory of the Nazi horror."[181] Poignant evidence of this preoccupation is found in the dedication with which Levinas begins *Otherwise than Being or Beyond Essence*: "To the memory of those who were closest among the six million assassinated by the National Socialists, and of the millions on millions of all confessions and all nations, victims of the same hatred of the other man, the same anti-semitism."[182] With this memory ever in view, Levinas turns not to the Holy Nothingness, but to the infinite moral demand encountered in the face of the Other. As we have done before, we must ask what is to be made of this sort of difference, considering the fact that Rubenstein and Levinas seem to begin at the same place. It is this question that leads us on to the next chapter.

The One and the Many

Chapter 4

"Everything is full of gods." So said the Greek philosopher Thales, and one might be tempted to agree with him after confronting the plethora of different theologies that the world's religious thinkers have to offer. In our sample of thinkers who appear to accede to the demands of the *logos* formula, we considered eight different theologies: Whitehead, Rahner, Soloveitchik, Cone, Ruether, Rubenstein, Nāgārjuna, and Levinas each set forth a different view of the divine. This kind of diversity represents a challenge to theology as a discipline, for it calls into question the possibility of genuine theological knowledge. It is bad enough, a critic might say, that theologians cannot agree upon the specifics of the *how* of theological thinking. But there is no general agreement among theologians even about theology's *what*! Who ever heard of a discipline with no definite object to investigate, or a way of thinking with no particular subject matter? Theologians have been speculating about the divine for centuries and yet seem to have no secure knowledge to show for it.

Given the seriousness of the problem of theological pluralism, it seems clear that one of the tasks of contemporary theological thinking must be to search for some unity beneath the confusing manyness of theological proposals. This quest for the one in the many is not ancillary to other theological tasks, it is not a side issue to be handed over to those who prefer methodological hairsplitting to the actual practice of theological thinking. For the question as to the possibility of theological knowledge cannot be satisfactorily answered unless theologians can deal with the problem of theological pluralism.

The purpose of this chapter is to explore how theologians might respond to the challenge of contemporary theological pluralism or manyness. We shall consider four different options available to contemporary thinkers. Each of the four options is reasonable and serious, and in order to give all of them a fair hearing, each option will be argued as forcefully as possible. It must be emphasized that there may be other options in addition to the four positions that we shall examine here. These four positions do, however, represent a systematic progression: the first holds that *no theology can provide knowledge of the divine*; the second maintains that *one theology can provide knowledge of the divine*; the third asserts that *many theologies can provide knowledge of the divine*; the fourth claims that, *although no theology can provide knowledge of the divine, the task of theology can be reformulated*.

The first option is *skepticism*. It entails the conclusion that the theological enterprise should be ended, since theological knowledge is not possible. Recall that modernity and post-modernity generate a strong external skepticism about the possibility of knowing the infinite. According to the advocate of the first option, this skepticism is only strengthened by a look at the results of theological thinking. The skeptic might put it this way: "Given the contemporary worldview, we have reason to be suspicious about the ability to come to know the divine. Indeed, we are suspicious even about the existence of the divine. But it would be unreasonable to reject the possibility of theological knowledge without considering what those who believe such knowledge is possible have to say. When we do look at the fruits of theological investigation, we see only confusion. Thus, theologians themselves provide us with all the evidence we need to firmly reject the possibility of theological knowledge."

In Chapter Two, we considered the powerful justification of theological skepticism provided by Immanuel Kant in his *Critique of Pure Reason*. Genuine theoretical knowledge, said Kant, requires both a material element—the data given us by sensible intuition—and a formal element—the organizing structures provided by the mind. Theoretical knowledge of God is impossible, for the material element is always absent when we attempt to know God: an infinite reality can never be given in sensible intuition. Thus, we are left with only the idea of God, an idea that will always be empty. In a section of the *Critique of Pure Reason* that he titles "Transcendental Dialectic," Kant attempts to show how the use of ideas devoid of the content provided by sensible intuition necessarily leads to illusion. He argues, for instance, that the use of such empty ideas will result in positions that contradict one another, even though each position is arrived at through reasoning that appears logical.

For the skeptic, our sample of theological positions in

Chapter Three is a concrete exemplification of Kant's warnings. Whitehead, Rahner, Soloveitchik, Cone, Ruether, Rubenstein, Nāgārjuna, and Levinas each advanced a carefully crafted theology consonant with the demand for a universally available account of the *how* and the *what* of theological knowledge. Yet their versions of the divine ranged from Cone's personal God who becomes incarnate in the man Jesus and intervenes in human history to free the oppressed, to Nāgārjuna's emptiness. Thus, it turns out that abstract philosophical arguments about the impossibility of theology, Kantian or otherwise, are buttressed by the actual failure of theological thinking. In addition, it should be noted that the apparent disarray of contemporary theology is not simply a function of conflict between different religious confessions; the problem cannot be traced, for example, to the fact that Jewish theologians present a Jewish perspective and Christian theologians a Christian one. Rather, there is great diversity *within* a single confession: the God of Soloveitchik is very different from that of Rubenstein, and Rahner's God is surely not the same as Ruether's.

The skeptic's conclusion that the pathway of theological thinking is a dead end will, of course, hardly appeal to theologians. But however unappealing the theologian finds this first option for addressing the apparent confusion within theology, he or she must acknowledge that it has a certain plausibility. Hence, the theologian is challenged to come up with something better than, or at least something as good as, the skeptical option.

The second option can be designated, simply enough, as the way of *selection*. One can argue that, while many different kinds of theology observe the general tenets of the *logos* formula, it is nonetheless reasonable to select one particular theological position as more adequate than the others. True, we may be frustrated that, despite its long history, theology has been unable to produce agreement about just which position to select. We should not, however, be surprised at this fact. After all, theology seeks the infinite, not some entity that, as a part of the finite world, can be hauled into the laboratory for definitive analysis. Theologians have always known that their thinking provokes God to laughter.

From time to time we have had occasion to point to similarities between Martin Heidegger's notion of the way of thinking that leads to Being, and theology as a way of thinking that leads to the divine. It is illuminating, therefore, to apply John Macquarrie's assessment of the later Heidegger to theology. Macquarrie notes that Heidegger's analysis of the meaning of Being is elusive and not entirely clear. Then he asks, "But could it be otherwise? Could one do more than evoke Being? The very point that Being (*Sein*, *esse*) is not itself a being (*Seiendes*, *ens*) and is indeed wholly other to beings [recall that this distinction is crucial for Heidegger] entails that one could never answer—at least, in any straightforward way—the question, 'What is Being?' For this very question implies that Being 'is' a 'what' or a 'something'."[183] Wouldn't this apply just as well to the theological quest? As a matter of fact, in the estimation of someone like Nāgārjuna, the infinite is probably even more elusive than Being. Levinas clearly holds this to be so.

If we grant that theological thinking cannot be expected to issue in the same kind of agreement as do disciplines with more mundane objects, the way of selection nonetheless requires that we can specify reasonable ways to argue for the superiority of one position over others. The advocate of selection will have no difficulty in rising to this challenge. For instance, one might argue that a particular theological position preempts all others because of the absolute priority of its starting point. Levinas again comes to mind, for he will point out that the infinity of my moral responsibility to the Other antedates any experience of Being, which most other theologies equate with *theos*: the Other has always already passed by the temporal horizon in which I try to unify the world and think Being.

Another reasonable way to proceed in justifying one's selection of a particular theology would be to offer some kind of systematic analysis of the whole theological landscape. In other words, one could begin by organizing the apparent jumble of theological proposals into a number of basic categories. This would serve to simplify one's theological choices; there would no longer be a seemingly infinite number of theologies from which to choose, but only a few basic types. Furthermore, the advocate of a particular theological position could focus on the classificatory principles as the key to the superiority of his or her own proposal: "Here we have the basic types of theology, and type 'x' is superior to all others insofar as type 'x' is characterized by such and such a property, which the other types lack."

As a concrete example of this kind of procedure,

consider Charles Hartshorne's article on "The Formally Possible Doctrines of God." Hartshorne, one of the best known advocates of a Whiteheadian process theology, boils down the various theologies available to us into three basic types, types arrived at by considering the possible ways in which God can be said to be perfect. This expedites both the exposition of his position and the argument that his position is superior to others: "We shall see presently that it [Hartshorne's position] *must* be an expression of one of the three and only three formally possible views regarding the supreme being. . . .it is related to the two other possible views as a 'higher synthesis' to its 'thesis' and 'antithesis,' as embraced and corrected in a 'higher unity,' or as a balanced whole truth to its two contrasting half-truths."[184] Thus, Hartshorne's selection of one theological position over others is not simply arbitrary.

Another classificatory system, one that operates at a more fundamental level and is more inclusive than Hartshorne's discussion of divine perfection, is provided by Robert Scharlemann in *The Being of God* (as the quotation above indicates, Hartshorne's scheme covers only the notion of "the supreme being," while Scharlemann's can encompass other notions of the divine as well). Scharlemann holds that there are three basic ways in which we can understand the assertion, "God is."[185] On the basis of this tripartite classification, he is able not only to reduce the theological landscape to manageable proportions, but also to assess the strengths and weaknesses of various theological proposals in a systematic, rather than an offhand, fashion. As a result, Scharlemann's selection of a particular theological perspective is clearly reasonable.

Of course, to say that the procedures adopted by Hartshorne and Scharlemann make their selections reasonable is not the same as claiming that it renders them unavoidable or indisputable. Once again, the infinite is not subject to laboratory experiment; there can be no such thing as indubitable theological proof. As Hartshorne puts it, ". . . men do not adopt a philosophy because its proofs are beyond question and its conclusions completely satisfactory—this being never the case—but because its proofs seem to them stronger and its conclusions more satisfactory than would be true of what they regard as the alternative. It is a question of preference, not of absolute sunclear evidence and perfect understanding."[186] Furthermore, it would be naive to expect that everyone will agree even about which theological position out of the many possible positions is preferable to the rest; we possess neither indisputable proof for the truth of a particular theology nor indisputable standards for judging one theology more satisfactory than others. Thus, while we must demand that theologians subject themselves to the dictates of reason and the principles contained in the *logos* formula, we cannot maintain that it is legitimate for them to advance or select a particular position only if they can convince all others of the wisdom of their choice.

The third option is to adopt what we shall call a *world theology*.[187] Perhaps the manyness of contemporary theological proposals can be taken up into an ultimate oneness in a literal sense. In other words, maybe there is some way of showing that many, if not all, of the serious theological positions that adhere to the demands of the *logos* formula ultimately point to the same divine reality. How would a world theology be constructed? A modest beginning might be made simply by looking for ways in which one theology could learn from others. Perhaps some apparently contradictory theological notions are in fact complementary. A good example of this approach is John Cobb's *Beyond Dialogue: Toward a Mutual Transformation of Christianity and Buddhism*. Cobb explores the potential complementarity of a Whiteheadian process interpretation of Christianity and Buddhism. He suggests, for instance, that Christian theology as he understands it can incorporate Buddhist insights on the nature of the self, time, and ultimate reality.

It bears repeating at this point that theological diversity is not simply a function of the existence of different religious traditions. While Cobb's exploration of complementarity brings together different religions, there is no reason to limit such exploration to interreligious matters; intrareligious diversity deserves consideration as well. Thus, when we speak of a world theology, we have in mind a theology that can embrace not just the different world religions, but also the kind of general theological diversity evident in our sample in Chapter Three. After all, from the perspective of an academic theology, confessional divisions are not of overriding significance.

But we cannot be certain that we shall arrive at a genuine world theology merely by looking for complementary features in different theological positions. As suggested at the outset, a world theology in the fullest sense will involve the contention that diverse theologies actually point to a single divine reality. At least this much can be said, then: if the way of complementarity is to result in a world theology, it must uncover a fundamental harmony not among just any portions of the diverse theologies it explores, but specifically among their various conceptions of *theos*.

Let us turn to what might might be called a "negative world theology" (negative because it emphasizes what we do not and cannot know about the divine). Negative world theology works this way: although my own theology seems to point to a different sort of divinity from those intended by other theologies, I recognize that I can grasp the divine only in a very imperfect fashion; I am sensitive to the laughter of God. Thus, I hypothesize that the differences among theologies are a function not of the various theologies pointing to different divinities, only one of which can exist, but of the imperfection of each theology's way of apprehending the one divine reality. An analogy is provided by the familiar story of the blind men and the elephant: one man, grasping the elephant's tail, says that an elephant is like a rope. Another, touching a leg, counters that an elephant is more like a tree. A third man holds the trunk, and he asserts that an elephant is much like a snake. The point, of course, is that all three are right to a certain extent, and that none of them understands the nature of an elephant in its entirety.

But there is a difficulty inherent in the negative form of world theology. Precisely because I do not really know the nature of the divine, I am in no position to claim that various theologies all point to it; only one who does know the characteristics of *theos* can judge that a particular theology points to *theos*, whether perfectly or imperfectly. A blind man cannot determine whether his blind companions are truly touching an elephant; only a sighted man who clearly observes what is happening can decide that.

Thus, we are led to what we shall call a "positive world theology." Such a theology is built on the assumption that one has sufficient knowledge of the divine to recognize both *that* other theologies grasp the divine and *how* they grasp it. Indeed, the recognition *that* may well rest upon the recognition of *how*. As an example, consider a world theology based on the thought of Karl Rahner. Recall Rahner's claim that all persons, given the very nature of human consciousness, have a preapprehension of unlimited being and that this amounts to an unthematic knowledge of God. A

Rahnerian has grounds, then, for saying that, whatever method a theologian may choose, he or she will always begin with at least a dim awareness of the reality of God. And note that our hypothetical Rahnerian is not necessarily beyond earshot of God's laughter. Even a positive world theology can incorporate an element of humility, for while one may have sufficient knowledge of the divine to judge that other theologies too know the divine and to recognize how they know it, it is nonetheless true that one does not fully comprehend the divine reality. And once it has been admitted both that other theologies grasp the divine and that one's own theology does not entail complete understanding of the divine reality, the possibility arises that those other theologies may possess insights about God unavailable from one's own vantage point. On some counts, of course, the Rahnerian's vision of God will inevitably be clearer than that of others—recall that our example presupposes that we are looking at things from the Rahnerian's perspective—for he or she is the one who realizes from whence knowledge of God arises, viz., the preapprehension of infinite being that underlies all human thinking and acting. But perhaps other thinkers, while not as fully cognizant of the *source* of their awareness of God, have found better ways to interpret that awareness. Is it not conceivable, for example, that while the most immediate access to God is, as Rahner suggests, found in the preapprehension of unlimited being, there are nonetheless some ways in which Rosemary Radford Ruether's theology more adequately conceives the nature of God than does Rahner's theology? For instance, Ruether's use of the insights of the sociology of knowledge (which shows how thinking is conditioned by its social context) and, in particular, her recognition of how patriarchy has skewed our notions of God, may afford her a perspective simply unavailable to Rahner. Surely the Rahnerian cannot dismiss this possibility out of hand.

Yet another approach to a world theology is suggested by the discovery that many theologies point to a transformative power that conquers ontic, moral, and spiritual anxiety. These theologies display *theos* concretely: they uncover something that must be deemed infinite insofar as it can negate the negativites inherent in human finitude. We found this kind of display in the theologies of Soloveitchik, Cone, Ruether, Rubenstein, and Nāgārjuna (and recall that Rahner and Whitehead advanced theologies that implied the existence of such a power, but reference to this power was not a crucial step in their theological arguments). Couldn't one claim, then, that despite the profound conceptual differences among these various theologies, they all point to the same infinite reality, practically speaking? In other words, it might be possible to construct a world theology by analyzing the empowerment to which various theological positions point.[188]

Perhaps there are other avenues to a world theology in addition to those discussed here. On the other hand, perhaps no world theology will ever thrive unless there exists a unified, world culture in which it can take root. In any case, if a healthy world theology were to emerge, it would have the notable virtue of demonstrating that the diversity within theology points not to the poverty of theological knowledge, but to a wealth of perspectives on one infinite reality.

The fourth option begins where the skeptic begins, with the conclusion that God as ordinarily conceived does not exist, or that, at the very least, we have no way of knowing whether there is a God. But this fourth way, which we shall call the way of *construction*, holds that the task of theology can be reformulated. While there is no independently existing divine reality, we can construct or create the divine. That is, we can formulate a notion of God or the infinite and use it as a symbol to orient our thinking and acting.

The masters of suspicion inspired by Feuerbach— Marx, Nietzsche, and Freud are the most important examples—critique the religious impulse by suggesting that God is a human creation. But they hold that much of the evil caused by religion results from the fact that we do not realize that God is our own creation; we interpret God as an independent entity and are thereby trapped in a destructive illusion. By contrast, theological construction as we are envisioning it here is a self-conscious act of creation, the formulation of a guiding symbol which we recognize as a symbol.

If we turn once more to the "Transcendental Dialectic" in Kant's *Critique of Pure Reason*, we will find Kant suggesting that, as a guide for our thinking, we can formulate an idea of a God who is a perfect unity and who has created the universe as a unified, rational whole. This God-idea can be used to regulate our thinking, even though we shall never actually experience any such deity. It is an ideal that challenges us to attempt to see the universe as thoroughly intelligible and prods us to seek ever more encompassing, more unified explanations of the universe.

Kant's reflections in the *Critique of Pure Reason* provide a starting point for a discussion of the way of construction, but the theologian will have to construct a God-symbol that touches more practical, existential issues, such as the anxieties resulting from our finitude. Thus, the theologian might consider the position taken by the American philosopher, John Dewey. Dewey denies the existence of a supernatural world beyond the world of nature. There is no God if God be conceived as a Supreme Being. But Dewey does have an important place for God as symbol: the word "God" denotes the unity of all our ideal ends, along with the conditions in nature and society that make the realization of those ends a possibility. Is Dewey's God "unreal"? Not at all, for ideals have a very real effect upon us. In fact, "ends, purposes, exercise determining power in human conduct."[189] Furthermore, the kind of ideals Dewey has in mind are rooted in the genuine possibilities provided us by the real world of which we are a part. A similar proposal is advanced by the Jewish thinker Mordecai Kaplan, according to whom "The word 'God' has. . . come to be symbolically expressive of the highest ideals for which men strive and, at the same time, points to the objective fact that the world is so constituted as to make for the realization of those ideals."[190]

More recent examples of a constructivist approach to theology are provided by the work of the British theologian, Don Cupitt—he holds that "God is a unifying symbol that eloquently personifies and represents to us everything that spirituality requires of us,"[191] and that "theological realism," the view that God exists independently of our imagination, is a "crude mistake"[192]—and American theologian Gordon Kaufman, who has written a book subtitled *Constructing the Concept of God*[193] (though Kaufman sometimes seems unsure whether God is entirely our own creation).

Theological pluralism is a problem because it suggests confusion about what is really "out there." The way of construction eliminates this problem by suggesting that theology is not about something "out there." Rather, it is a matter of self-consciously constructing God as a guiding symbol. If there were many constructivist theologies, that would not mean that theologians were confused about what exists, but only that they were proposing different God-symbols.

The way of construction is attractive not only because

it appears to solve the problem of theological pluralism, but also because it suggests a way of doing theology after skepticism has taken its toll. But many persons feel that the constructivist approach gives up too much to skepticism and leaves us with an impotent, all-too-human deity. Thus, the way of construction is both a fascinating and a controversial option for theological thinking.

If we now look back over the ground we have covered in this chapter, it is apparent that we began with a position which holds that no theology can provide knowledge of the divine, we moved to a position which maintains that one theology can provide knowledge of the divine, we then turned to a position which asserts that many theologies can provide knowledge of the divine, and we concluded with a position that claims that, while no theology can provide knowledge of the divine, the task of theology can be meaningfully reformulated. The first option, *skepticism*, entails the end of theology. But it is an option that can be reasonably argued, and, as such, it must be taken seriously by theologians. The second, third, and fourth options provide different ways for theologians to confront the pluralism that currently characterizes their discipline.

The way of *selection* points to the difficulty of knowing the infinite. It shows that the theologian is justified in advancing one particular position even though he or she can demonstrate neither the indubitability of that position nor the untenability of all other proposals. For God is always, to some degree, what theologians have traditionally designated a *deus absconditus*, a hidden God.

A *world theology* takes up the manyness of contemporary theological discussion into a higher unity. It argues that many of the diverse theological proposals that exist today represent different perspectives on the same divine reality. The task before one who wants to advance a world theology is to show not just what the many theologies share as their common object of knowledge, but also how they can all know it despite their often very different vantage points. Or, as an alternative, one could perhaps advance a world theology by showing how many theologies point to the same transformative power.

The way of *construction* begins by denying that we do or can possess any knowledge of an actually existing divinity. It then reformulates the role of theology: the theologian's task is to construct a God-symbol to guide our thinking and acting. The problem of theological pluralism disappears, for the existence of many theologies is no longer a function of confusion about what sort of divinity exists, but the result of a diversity of opinions about what sort of God-symbol is most useful.

Why Does It Matter?

Chapter 5

Perhaps no retort to an idea that one has put forward for discussion is more devastating than, "So what?" Even an expression of vehement disagreement is preferable, for that suggests that one's idea is at least being taken seriously. Suppose, then, that someone were to reply to the whole theological enterprise with, "So what?" Why does the discipline called theology matter? This is the question we must address by way of conclusion to our investigation.

Theology matters, first, because *the issues that it explores matter*. We have noted that theology seeks to know an infinite reality that can deliver human beings from ontic, moral, and spiritual anxiety. Thus, theology deals with questions that can only be called "ultimate ": Is it possible for human beings to face their own finitude, to face the fact that they are subject to forces which they cannot control and which will result, finally, in their death? Can human beings live their lives as they believe they ought to be lived, given the essence of what it means to be human, or must they inevitably incur the guilt of having fallen short? Is human existence ultimately meaningful, or must it always be lived amidst the despair of emptiness and meaninglessness?

Theology matters, second, because *it approaches such ultimate questions via a disciplined way of thinking*. One could, of course, answer life's ultimate questions simply on the basis of one's emotional needs, or on the basis of what one has been taught to believe. One could make a leap of faith, or of unbelief, without engaging in rational reflection. And it is always possible to deceive oneself about one's reasons for accepting or rejecting a particular perspective on life's ultimate questions. For example, Abraham Heschel has noted that "religious thinking, believing, feeling are among the most deceptive activites of the human spirit. We often assume it is God we believe in, but in reality it may be a symbol of personal interests that we dwell upon. We may assume that we feel drawn to God, but in reality it may be a power within the world that is the object of our adoration. We may assume it is God we care for, but it may be our own ego we are concerned with. To examine our religious existence is, therefore, a task to be performed constantly."[194] Theology as we have described it is not necessarily a function of religious belief. But theology analyzes issues central to religious belief and practice, and, as a disciplined way of thinking, it is useful in uncovering the sort of self-deception described by Heschel.

Theology matters, third, because *it offers a distinctive kind of answer to man and woman's ultimate questions*: whatever the specifics of its notion of the divine—they range from Rahner's Trinitarian God to Dewey's symbol of our ideal ends—theology addresses the dilemmas posed by human finitude by pointing to something that transcends our present finite existence. Theology points to *theos*, to the infinite. Perhaps theology is mistaken in this regard. It may be that the only viable answer to the fundamental dilemmas inherent in finitude is for each of us to eschew any notion of the infinite and to look instead to our own individual resources. Maybe the doctor in Ralph Ellison's *Invisible Man* has it right when he says, "Be your own father."[195] But it is safe to say that we cannot be certain that this advice is well taken unless we have considered the alternatives, and precisely because theology proposes a worldview significantly different from the kind defended in Ellison's novel, it is important to consider what theology has to say. Our reflection about the world in which we find ourselves is incomplete unless it at least considers the particular perspective afforded by theological thinking.

Theology matters, finally, because *it is a source of intellectual delight*. Even if we cannot be certain that humanity's drive to know the infinite results in genuine knowledge rather than in illusion, we cannot but sense the beauty of the patterns traced by the human mind in its quest for what is beyond the finite. And while a careful reading of Thomas Aquinas' *Summa Theolgiae* or of Franz Rosenzweig's *Star of Redemption* requires disciplined concentration, such concentration is inevitably rewarded: we discover that, at its best, theological thinking is characterized by both an artful intricacy and an exhilirating breadth of vision.

Notes

[1] Paul Tillich, *The Courage to Be* (New Haven: Yale University Press, 1952), pp. 32-63.

[2] Leo Baeck, *The Essence of Judaism* (New York: Schoken, 1948), p. 142.

[3] Quoted in Schubert M. Ogden, *On Theology* (San Francisco: Harper and Row, 1986), p. 3.

[4] Frederick J. Streng, Charles L. Lloyd, Jr., and Jay T. Allen, *Ways of Being Religious* (Englewood Cliffs, NJ: Prentice Hall, 1973), p. 6.

[5] Hermann Cohen, *Religion of Reason out of the Sources of Judaism*, trans. Simon Kaplan (New York: Frederick Ungar, 1972), p. 82.

[6] Paul Tillich, *Systematic Theology*, 3 vols. (Chicago: University of Chicago Press, 1951-63), 1:60.

[7] Ibid., pp. 61-62.

[8] David Tracy, *Blessed Rage for Order: The New Pluralism in Theology* (New York: Seabury, 1975), p. 43; 45.

[9] Ogden, *On Theology*, p. 9.

[10] I am construing the notion of correlation broadly enough that it can be applied to a wide range of theologies. It is important to note that even theologians who openly refer to their own methods as "correlative" do not always approve of how correlation is used by others. For example, David Tracy has serious difficulties with some aspects of Paul Tillich's use of correlation (see *Blessed Rage for Order*, p. 46.) Furthermore, the notion of correlation sometimes has more than one meaning even within the work of a single theologian. A number of studies have pointed out, for instance, that Paul Tillich's method of correlation has more than one form. See, e.g., John Powell Clayton, *The Concept of Correlation: Paul Tillich and the Possibility of a Mediating Theology* (Berlin: Walter De Gruyter, 1980).

[11] For a difficult but important proposal about how theology as a way of thinking should be contrasted with Heidegger's way of thinking Being, see Robert P. Scharlemann, "Being Open and Thinking Theologically," in *Unfinished. . . Essays in Honor of Ray L. Hart*, ed. Mark C. Taylor, JAAR Thematic Series (Atlanta: Scholars Press, 1981), pp. 111-124.

[12] J. Glenn Gray, "Introduction," in Martin Heidegger, *What is Called Thinking?* trans. J. Glenn Gray (New York: Harper and Row, 1968), p. xi.

[13] In the English-speaking world, the word "science" tends to be synonomous with the *natural* sciences. The word is being used here in its European sense, signifying the more general notion of an organized discipline or way of inquiry.

[14] Peter Berger, *The Sacred Canopy: Elements of a Sociological Theory of Religion* (Garden City, NY: Doubleday-Anchor, 1967), p. 107.

[15] See Robert N. Bellah, "The Triumph of Secularism," *Religion and Intellectual Life* 1 (winter 1984): 13-26.

[16] Ibid., p. 16.

[17] Berger, *The Sacred Canopy*, p. 107.

[18] Ibid., p. 138.

[19] See Ibid., p. 138.

[20] Eugene Borowitz, *Choices in Modern Jewish Thought: A Partisan Guide* (New York: Behrman House, 1983), p. 5.

[21] Quoted in Ibid., p. 8.

[22] Immanuel Kant, *Critique of Pure Reason*, trans. Norman Kemp Smith (New York: St. Martin's Press, 1965), p. 22.

[23] Ibid., p. 646.

[24] Charles Hartshorne and William L. Reese, *Philosophers Speak of God* (Chicago: University of Chicago Press, 1953), p. 448.

[25] Ludwig Feuerbach, *The Essence of Christianity*, trans. George Eliot (New York: Harper and Row, 1957), p. xxxvii.

[26] James Cone, *God of the Oppressed* (New York: Seabury, 1975), p. 46.

[27] See Richard Rubenstein, *The Cunning of History: Mass Death and the American Future* (New York: Harper and Row, 1975).

[28] Cf. David Tracy's similar analysis of the transition from the modern period to the postmodern in *Blessed Rage for Order*, pp. 8, 10-14. A much more radical interpretation of postmodernism is set forth by contemporary French theorists such as Jacques Derrida. Students with significant preparation in recent philosophy and/or literary criticism may wish to explore the theological appropriation of this radical postmodernism in works such as Thomas J.J. Altizer, et al., *Deconstruction and Theology* (New York: Crossroad, 1982); Mark C. Taylor, *Erring: A Postmodern A/Theology* (Chicago: University of Chicago Press, 1984); Charles E. Winquist, *Epiphanies of Darkness: Deconstruction in Theology* (Philadelphia: Fortress, 1986).

[29] Philip Larkin, "Church Going," in *The Less*

Deceived: *Poems by Philip Larkin* (New York: St. Martin's Press, 1960), pp. 28-29.

[30]David Kelsey, *The Uses of Scripture in Recent Theology* (Philadelphia: Fortress, 1975), pp. 134-5.

[31]Karl Barth, *The Epistle to the Romans*, trans. Edwyn C. Hoskyns (London: Oxford University Press, 1968), p. 10.

[32]Ibid., pp. 29-30.

[33]Ibid., p. 367.

[34]Hans Urs von Balthasar, *The Theology of Karl Barth*, trans. John Drury (Garden City, NY: Doubleday-Anchor, 1972), p. 83.

[35]Karl Barth, *Church Dogmatics*, 4 vols., trans. G.W. Bromiley (Edinburgh: T. and T. Clark, 1936-69), I/1, 2nd edition: 238.

[36]Ibid., p. 243.

[37]Ibid., p. 244.

[38]Ibid., p. 238.

[39]Quoted in von Balthasar, *The Theology of Karl Barth*, p. 90.

[40]Karl Barth, *Anselm*: *Fides Quaerens Intellectum*, trans. Ian W. Robertson (Cleveland: World-Meridian, 1962), p. 39.

[41]Ibid., p. 170.

[42]Cf. Robert P. Scharlemann's assessment of Barth according to which, while the Anselmian formula does *not* presuppose a leap of faith, there does exist a gap between the reality of God presented in Anselm's formula and the Christian Bible, which Barth takes to be the definitive witness to God's revelation. See "The No to Nothing and the Nothing to Know: Barth and Tillich on the Possibility of Theological Science," *Journal of the American Academy of Religion* 55 (spring 1987): 57-72.

[43]Barth, *Church Dogmatics*, I/1: 222.

[44]John B. Cobb, *Living Options in Protestant Theology*: *A Survey of Methods* (Philadelphia: Westminster, 1962), p. 197.

[45]Barth, *Church Dogmatics*, I/1: 222.

[46]Ibid., p. 189.

[47]Ibid., p. 188.

[48]Quoted in Wolfhart Pannenberg, *Theology and the Philosophy of Science*, trans. Francis McDonagh (Philadelphia: Westminster, 1976), p. 272.

[49]Ibid., p. 273.

[50]Alfred North Whitehead, *Process and Reality*: *An Essay on Cosmology* (New York: Harper and Row, 1957), p. 525.

[51]Ibid., p. 527.

[52]Ibid., p. 529.

53 Ibid., pp. 15-16.

54 Ibid., p. 252.

55 Ibid., p. 135.

56 Ibid., pp. 27-28.

57 Ibid., pp. 69-70.

58 John B. Cobb, *A Christian Natural Theology Based on the Thought of Alfred North Whitehead* (Philadelphia: Westminster, 1965), p. 34.

59 Whitehead, *Process and Reality*, p. 521.

60 Ibid., p. 524.

61 Alfred North Whitehead, *Religion in the Making* (New York: New American Library-Meridian, 1954), 68-69.

62 Whitehead, *Process and Reality*, p. 377.

63 Karl Rahner, *Foundations of Christian Faith: An Introduction to the Idea of Christianity*, trans. William V. Dych (New York: Seabury, 1978), p. 219.

64 Ibid., p. 63.

65 Karl Rahner, *A Rahner Reader*, ed. Gerald A. McCool (New York: Seabury, 1975), p. 121.

66 Rahner, *Foundations of Christian Faith*, p. 225.

67 Ibid., p. 221.

68 Ibid., p. 305.

69 On Rahner's rejection of Hegelian panentheism, see *A Rahner Reader*, p. 11. But cf. p. xxvii, where Gerald McCool points out that Rahner has been interpreted as advancing a form of panentheism based on the philosophy of Thomas Aquinas.

70 Rahner, *Foundations of Christian Faith*, p. 241.

71 Ibid., p. 230.

72 Ibid., p. 231.

73 Ibid., p. 243.

74 Rahner, *A Rahner Reader*, p. 4.

75 Ibid., p. 15.

76 Rahner, *Foundations of Christian Faith*, p. 34.

77 Rahner, *A Rahner Reader*, p. 20.

78 See Martin Heidegger, *Being and Time*, trans. John Macquarrie and Edward Robinson (New York: Harper and Row, 1962).

79 Rahner, *Foundations of Christian Faith*, p. 35.

80 Ibid., p. 155.

81 Ibid., p. 194.

82 Ibid., p. 225.

83 For an overview of Soloveitchik that goes beyond *Halakhic Man* and indicates the difficulty of discerning a unified perspective in his work taken as a whole, see Borowitz, *Choices in Modern Jewish Thought*, pp. 218-242.

84 Joseph Soloveitchik, *Halakhic Man*, trans. Lawrence

Kaplan (Philadelphia: Jewish Publication Society of
America, 1983), p. 142.

85Ibid., p. 5.

86See Ibid., p. 13.

87See Rudolf Otto, *The Idea of the Holy*, trans. John
W. Harvey (London: Oxford University Press, 1950).

88See Soloveitchik, *Halakhic Man*, p. 68.

89Ibid., p 41.

90Ibid., p. 43.

91Ibid., p. 141.

92Cf. Richard Rubenstein's articulation of the opposite
position, viz., that calculative reason was partly responsible for the Nazi Holocaust (see note 27, above).

93Soloveitchik, *Halakhic Man*, p. 20.

94Ibid., p. 59.

95Ibid., pp. 41-2.

96Ibid., p. 30.

97Ibid., p. 99.

98Ibid., p. 101.

99Ibid., p. 109.

100Ibid., p. 110. Cf. Pinchas Peli, *Soloveitchik On
Repentance* (New York: Paulist Press, 1984).

101For a phenomenology of Christian existence parallel
to (though not influenced by) Soloveitchik's *Halakhic
Man*, see Edward Farley, *Ecclesial Man: A Social
Phenomenology of Faith and Reality* (Philadelphia: Fortress, 1975).

102Steve Gowler, "Liberation Theology: An Introduction to Its History and Themes," *Counseling and Values*
31 (October 1986): 4-5.

103James Cone, *God of the Oppressed* (New York:
Seabury, 1975).

104Ibid., p. 133.

105Ibid., p. 135.

106For a different view of the place of existential issues
in black theology, see Cornel West, *Prophesy Deliverance!
An Afro-American Revolutionary Christianity* (Philadelphia: Westminster, 1982), p. 106.

107Cone, *God of the Oppressed*, p. 132.

108Ibid., p. 143.

109Rosemary Radford Ruether, *Sexism and God-Talk:
Toward a Feminist Theology* (Boston: Beacon Press,
1983), pp. 68-9.

110Ibid., p. 49.

111Ibid., p. 157.

112Ibid., p. 138.

113Ibid., p. 255.

114Ibid., p. 163.

115Brown lays out the six characteristics in *Theology in*

a New Key (Philadelphia: Westminster, 1978), pp. 60-74. Long's summary is found in his *A Survey of Recent Christian Ethics* (New York: Oxford University Press, 1982), p. 159.

[116]e.g., *God of the Oppressed*, pp. 30-38.

[117]*Sexism and God-Talk*, pp. 12-13.

[118]Ibid., pp. 21-22.

[119]Cone, *God of the Oppressed*, p. 91.

[120]Ibid., p. 92.

[121]Ruether, *Sexism and God-Talk*, p. 41.

[122]See, for example, *My Soul Looks Back* (Nashville: Abingdon, 1982).

[123]Cone, *God of the Oppressed*, p. 219.

[124]Ibid., p. 17.

[125]Ruether, *Sexism and God-Talk*, pp. 18-19.

[126]Cone, *God of the Oppressed*, p. 99.

[127]Cornel West, "The Historicist Turn in Philosophy of Religion," in *Knowing Religiously*, ed. Leroy S. Rouner, Boston University Studies in Philosophy and Religion, vol. 7 (Notre Dame: University of Notre Dame Press, 1985), p. 45.

[128]Ralph Ellison, *Shadow and Act* (New York: Random House, 1964), p. 170.

[129]See note 122 above.

[130]This is one of the concerns evident in Cornel West's *Prophecy Deliverance*!

[131]Friedrich Nietzsche, *Joyful Wisdom*, trans. Thomas Common (New York: Frederick Ungar, 1960), pp. 167-9.

[132]Langdon Gilkey, *Naming the Whirlwind*: *The Renewal of God-Language* (Indianapolis: Bobbs-Merrill, 1969), p. 140.

[133]Richard L. Rubenstein, *After Auschwitz*: *Radical Theology and Contemporary Judaism* (Indianapolis: Bobbs-Merrill, 1966), p. x.

[134]Ibid., p. 240.

[135]Ibid., p. 123.

[136]Ibid., p. 125.

[137]Ibid., p. 258.

[138]Ibid., p. 140.

[139]See note 87 above.

[140]See Rubenstein, *After Auschwitz*, pp. 218-20.

[141]Ibid., p. 198.

[142]Ibid., p. 238.

[143]Ibid., p. 90.

[144]Ibid., pp. 128-9.

[145]Ibid. pp. 205-6.

[146]Cf. Louis Dupré's interpretation of Rubenstein in *The Other Dimension*: *A Search for the Meaning of Religious Attitudes* (New York: Seabury, 1979), p. 69.

147Antony Flew, "Theology and Falsification," in *New Essays in Philosophical Theology*, ed. Antony Flew and Alasdair MacIntyre (New York: Macmillan, 1955), p. 96.

148Jacob Neusner, "The Implications of the Holocaust," in *Understanding Jewish Theology*, ed. Jacob Neusner (New York: KTAV, 1973), p. 193.

149Richard L. Rubenstein, *The Religious Imagination*: *A Study in Psychoanalysis and Jewish Theology* (Indianapolis: Bobbs-Merrill, 1968), pp. xviii-xix.

150Frederick J. Streng, *Emptiness*: *A Study in Religious Meaning* (Nashville: Abingdon, 1967).

151Ibid., p. 18.

152Ibid., pp. 39-40.

153Ibid., p. 86.

154Ibid., p. 149.

155Quoted in Ibid., p. 56.

156Edward Conze, *Buddhism*: *Its Essence and Development* (New York: Harper and Row, 1959), p. 132.

157Ibid., p. 134.

158Frederick Copleston provides a carefully nuanced discussion of this view in *Religion and the One*: *Philosophies East and West* (New York: Crossroad, 1982), pp. 53-5.

159Quoted in Streng, *Emptiness*, p. 78.

160Ibid., p. 38.

161See Ibid., Chapter 11.

162Ibid., p. 166.

163Steven G. Smith, *The Argument to the Other*: *Reason Beyond Reason in the Thought of Karl Barth and Emmanuel Levinas*, AAR Academy Series, Number 42, ed. Carl Raschke (Chico, Calif: Scholars Press, 1983).

164Emmanuel Levinas, *Ethics and Infinity*: *Conversations with Phillippe Nemo*, trans. Richard A. Cohen (Pittsburgh: Duquesne University Press, 1985), p. 61.

165See Immanuel Kant, *Critique of Pure Reason*, pp. 135-61.

166Levinas, *Ethics and Infinity*, p. 60.

167In several of his works, Levinas points out his debt to Rosenzweig on this matter. See, for example, *Ethics and Infinity*, pp. 75-6. Rosenzweig's most important work, in which his opposition to totality is expressed, is his masterful *The Star of Redemption*, trans. William W. Hallo (Boston: Beacon Press, 1972).

168Emmanuel Levinas, *Otherwise than Being or Beyond Essence*, trans. Alphonso Lingis (The Hague: Martinus Nijhoff, 1981).

169Levinas, *Ethics and Infinity*, p. 105.

170Ibid., p. 88.

171Levinas makes this point frequently. See, for instance, *Otherwise than Being or Beyond Essence*, p. 142.

172Emmanuel Levinas, "God and Philosophy," trans. Richard Cohen, *Philosophy Today* 22 (summer 1978): 137.

173The classic expression of Buber's position is his *I and Thou*, trans. Walter Kaufmann (New York: Scribner's, 1970).

174Levinas, *Ethics and Infinity*, p. 106.

175The biblical passage in question is Genesis 3:8-13. Levinas refers to it in *Otherwise than Being or Beyond Essence*, p. 144.

176Levinas, "God and Philosophy," p. 145, n. 21.

177Smith, *The Argument to the Other*, p. 196.

178Cited in Ibid., p. 169.

179Levinas, *Otherwise than Being or Beyond Essence*, p. 150.

180Smith, *The Argument to the Other*, pp. 199-200.

181Quoted in Ibid., p. 285, n. 156.

182Levinas, *Otherwise than Being or Beyond Essence*, p. v.

183John Macquarrie, *Thinking About God* (New York: Harper and Row, 1975), pp. 195-6. For the sake of consistency with the references to "Being" in our previous discussions of Heidegger, I have taken the liberty of capitalizing "Being" (*Sein*) in this quotation from Macquarrie, even though Macquarrie himself does not.

184Charles Hartshorne, "The Formally Possible Doctrines of God," in *Process Philosophy and Christian Thought*, ed. Delwin Brown, Ralph E. James, Jr., and Gene Reeves (Indianapolis: Bobbs-Merrill, 1971), p. 189.

185Robert P. Scharlemann, *The Being of God: Theology and the Experience of Truth* (New York: Seabury, 1981), pp. 57-93.

186Hartshorne, "The Formally Possible Doctrines of God," p. 206.

187I take this phrase from Wilfred Cantwell Smith's *Towards a World Theology: Faith and the Comparative History of Religion* (Philadelphia: Westminster, 1981).

188Elsewhere I have attempted to describe in some detail an empowerment-oriented world theology based on the thought of Paul Tillich. See my *Symbol and Empowerment: Paul Tillich's Post-Theistic System* (Macon, GA: Mercer University Press, 1985).

189John Dewey, *A Common Faith* (New Haven: Yale University Press, 1934), p. 48.

190Mordecai M. Kaplan, *The Meaning of God in*

Modern Jewish Religion (New York: Reconstructionist Press, 1962), p. 306.

[191] Don Cupitt, *Taking Leave of God* (New York: Crossroad, 1981), p. 9.

[192] Ibid., p. 11.

[193] Gordon D. Kaufman, *The Theological Imagination*: *Constructing the Concept of God* (Philadelphia: Westminster, 1981).

[194] Abraham Joshua Heschel, *God in Search of Man*: *A Philosophy of Judaism* (New York: Meridian, 1959), p. 9.

[195] Ralph Ellison, *Invisible Man* (New York: Random House-Vintage, 1972), p. 154.

Suggestions for Further Reading

The works listed below should be reasonably accessible to persons just beginning to explore the world of theology. They have been arranged so as to indicate with which chapters in this book they most directly correspond.

Chapter One

Congar, Yves. "Christian Theology." In *The Encyclopedia of Religion*. Vol. 14, pp. 455-464. Mircea Eliade, Editor in Chief. New York: Macmillan, 1987.

Hodgson, Peter C. and King, Robert H., editors. *Christian Theology: An Introduction to Its Traditions and Tasks*. 2nd edition. Philadelphia: Fortress, 1985.

Jacobs, Louis. "Theology." In *Encyclopaedia Judaica*. Vol 15, pp. 1103-1110. Cecil Roth and Geoffrey Wigoder, Editors in Chief. New York: Macmillan, 1972.

Tillich, Paul. *The Courage to Be*. New Haven: Yale University Press, 1952.

Chapter Two

Berger, Peter. *The Sacred Canopy: Elements of a Sociological Theory of Religion*. Garden City, NY: Doubleday-Anchor, 1967.

Borowitz, Eugene. *Choices in Modern Jewish Thought: A Partisan Guide*. Chapter One: "The Challenge of Modernity to Judaism." New York: Behrman, 1983.

Feuerbach, Ludwig. *The Essence of Christianity*. Translated by George Eliot. New York: Harper and Row, 1957.

Freud, Sigmund. *The Future of an Illusion*. Translated by W.D. Robson-Scott. Revised and Edited by James Strachey. New York: Norton, 1975.

Körner, Stephan. *Kant*. New Haven: Yale University Press, 1982.

Marx, Karl and Engels, Friedrich. *On Religion*. Introduction by Reinhold Niebuhr. Chico, Calif: Scholars Press, 1982.

Chapter Three

Barth, Karl. *Church Dogmatics: A Selection.* Selected by Helmut Gollwitzer. Translated and Edited by G.W. Bromiley. New York: Harper and Row, 1962.

Cobb, John B. *A Christian Natural Theology Based on the Thought of Alfred North Whitehead.* Philadelphia: Westminster, 1965.

Cone, James. *God of the Oppressed.* New York: Seabury, 1975.

Levinas, Emmanuel. *Ethics and Infinity: Conversations with Phillippe Nemo.* Translated by Richard Cohen. Pittsburgh: Duquesne University Press, 1985.

Rahner, Karl. *Foundations of Christian Faith: An Introduction to the Idea of Christianity.* Translated by William V. Dych. New York: Seabury, 1978.

Rubenstein, Richard L. *After Auschwitz: Radical Theology and Contemporary Judaism.* Indianapolis: Bobbs-Merrill, 1966.

Ruether, Rosemary Radford. *Sexism and God-Talk: Toward a Feminist Theology.* Boston: Beacon Press, 1983.

Soloveitchik, Joseph. *Halakhic Man.* Translated by Lawrence Kaplan. Philadelphia: Jewish Publication Society of America, 1983.

Streng, Frederick J. *Emptiness: A Study in Religious Meaning.* Nashville: Abingdon, 1967. [an analysis of Nāgārjuna; the appendix contains translations of Nāgārjuna's "Fundamentals of the Middle Way" and "Averting the Arguments"].

Chapter Four

Cobb, John B. *Beyond Dialogue: Toward a Mutual Transformation of Christianity and Buddhism.* Philadelphia: Fortress, 1982.

Cupitt, Don. *Taking Leave of God.* New York: Crossroad, 1981.

Dewey, John. *A Common Faith.* New Haven: Yale University Press, 1934.

Hartshorne, Charles. "The Formally Possible Doctrines of God." In *Process Philosophy and Christian Thought.* Edited by Delwin Brown, Ralph E. James, Jr. and Gene Reeves. Indianapolis: Bobbs-Merrill, 1971.

Kaufman, Gordon D. *The Theological Imagination: Constructing the Concept of God.* Philadelphia: Westminster, 1981.

Smith, Wilfred Cantwell. *Towards a World Theology: Faith and the Comparative History of Religion.* Philadelphia: Westminster, 1981.

Schuon, Frithjof. *The Transcendent Unity of Religions.*

Revised Edition. Translated by Peter Townsend.
Introduction by Huston Smith. New York: Harper
and Row, 1975.
Tracy, David. "Comparative Theology." In *The
Encyclopedia of Religion*. Vol. 14, pp. 446-455.